GETTING BACK ON TRACK

REVITALIZE YOUR WALK WITH GOD

DR. BOB MOOREHEAD

GETTING BACK ON TRACK
© 1996 by Bob Moorehead

Published by Vision House Publishing, Inc.
1217 NE Burnside, Suite 403
Gresham, Oregon 97030

Edited by Jerry MacGregor

Printed in the United States of America.

International Standard Book Number: 1-885305-40-0

96 97 98 99 00 01 02 03 04 05 - 10 9 8 7 6 5 4 3 2 1

Printed in the United States by Morris Publishing
3212 East Highway 30
Kearney, NE 68847
1-800-650-7888

Contents
Getting Back on Track...

Foreword

THIS BOOK NEEDED TO BE WRITTEN. Since the Garden of Eden, men have been getting off track. No question about it. The problem for most of us lies in realizing and admitting we've gotten off track. That's why this book is so important.

It matters little if you are the CEO of a major corporation or a file clerk in a small office, this book is a word of truth and hope for every man. But truth is like soap; it won't do you any good unless it is applied.

When Adam sinned in the Garden of Eden, he hid from God out of fear and guilt. But God would not quit calling for Adam until he answered. When God asked him if he had eaten of the forbidden fruit, Adam ultimately blamed God for his sin by saying: "The woman you gave me...." Adam's refusal to accept responsibility for his actions constituted "denial."

Refusing to acknowledge his need is man's biggest barrier to change or help.

When Adam refused to admit he was wrong, it cost him his manhood and dignity. To this day that is still the reason many men never mature. A man is responsible for his success only if he is willing to be responsible for his failure.

Getting back on track, once off, is easier than it seems—one must simply be willing to admit his need for help.

Bob Moorehead writes not only of the predicament we may find ourselves in, but the answer to getting out of it. Anyone can make a mess, but it takes a willing person to clean it up. The first Adam in the garden refused to accept responsibility for his actions, but there came a LAST ADAM!

The Lord Jesus Christ not only accepted responsibility for His actions, but the actions of the entire world. By paying the price for man's sins, Christ made it possible for everyone to be changed eternally. Therein lies the real difference in men—those who cannot accept responsibility for their actions and those who accept it for themselves, their families, and others.

In the parable of the prodigal son there is a pattern of human life that Christ displayed for us all: rebellion, ruin, repentance, reconciliation, and restoration. The pivotal point between ruin and reconciliation is repentance, and repentance is simply being willing to change.

When getting off the track there is a way to get back on. Bob shows the way, the why, and the when. The result is a life of real manhood that only Christ gives.

Edwin Cole

Introduction

I WAS ALL OF TEN YEARS OLD when I received a Lionel electric train for Christmas. I was the proudest boy in the world—a real electric train! It literally had all the bells and whistles. When I put smoke pellets in the top of the engine, it blew smoke; when I pressed the right button, the train's whistle blew; when it crossed Main Street, the red signals went on. I was enthralled. There was just one problem. As the train would round the bend, it would jump the track almost every time. The culprit? Me. I was running the engine way too fast. So I slowed it down and never had that problem again.

Like that Lionel electric train, we tend to get "off track" when we go too fast. It doesn't happen all at once, but in a subtle way as our life speeds up, it gradually veers until we're completely off track. We wake up one morning and realize we're quite a distance from where we were...and very far from where we were headed!

Recently, I had breakfast with a man in that situation. I'll call him Fred to conceal his real identity. Most of us can identify with Fred. We met at his request early one morning and sat in the corner of a coffee shop for almost three hours. Fred's story could probably be repeated hundreds, even thousands of times. I certainly identified with what he told me. Let me repeat just the salient points:

1. At thirty-five, he was low on energy.
2. His marriage had lost its "zing." Even sex no longer interested him.
3. Though a huge success as regional manager of a large wholesaler, his job had ceased to challenge him.
4. His daily work outs at the health club dropped to twice a week, then to none at all.
5. He had trouble sleeping through the night.
6. He no longer had an interest in golf, though it once consumed him.
7. He made no investment in quiet time and prayer.
8. Though once active in church, now he attended only twice a month.
9. It was a challenge for him to get out of bed in the mornings.
10. He felt estranged from his wife and two children.

Fred had lost all the disciplines of his life. He was a long way from where he had been; a growing believer in Christ, excited about his church, his marriage, his family, his job, and his own spiritual growth. His first words to me that morning were, "Somewhere my life got off track, and I can't seem to get back on."

Our society is full of people who feel that way. This book is dedicated to those people who, like Fred, have gotten "off track" somewhere and need to get back on track and stay there. If you have your life together and are sensing no need for more growth, this book is not for you. You might want to give it to a friend. I tend, however, to think that if you've read just this far, you know that at least in some places, you need to get back on track.

Chapter One

Getting Back on Track Through Acknowledgment

A BUZZ PHRASE THESE DAYS IS "in denial." People addicted to drugs, alcohol, sex, and food are often referred to as "being in denial." This means they have a problem, but won't admit it.

I heard about Zeke, a cowboy who lived in Muleshoe, Texas. Proud, arrogant, and self-sufficient, he wandered into a blacksmith shop one day and, for want of anything better to do, picked up a horseshoe. He didn't know it had just come out of the fire. He quickly flung it down on the floor and yelled, "Ouch!" The blacksmith sheepishly grinned over the fact that Zeke had actually acknowledged pain and said, "What's wrong, Zeke? Too hot?" "Nope," Zeke answered back, "It just doesn't take me long to look at a horseshoe!"

I don't know about you, but there is a lot of Zeke in me. "Big boys don't cry," the old saying goes, to which I can add, "or ever admit they need something." Do you know why NASA finally decided to send women up in space ships? Because they aren't afraid to ask for directions when they're lost! (Ouch!) There is probably more truth than humor in that statement. I think most men would rather run out of gas in the Mojave Desert in 120 degree heat than admit they took the wrong road. There is something inside us that makes it very difficult to say we took a wrong turn, made a bad investment, used the wrong part, or gave the wrong information.

Remember Fred, the man I talked about in the introduction? He took a big step toward getting back on track the morning he met with me as his friend and pastor and acknowledged, "I got off track somewhere." That was hard for a six-foot-three-inch, good-looking, successful business man who had been at the top for a long time. It was like lancing a boil—painful, messy, traumatic, but oh so necessary for healing. The first thing you must do to get your life back on track is to acknowledge that it's off the rails. What are the steps of acknowledgment?

1. Assume full responsibility.

Blame-shifting is in vogue now. It's popular for people to explain away their behavior by claiming a dysfunctional family, some kind of abuse, or anything except personal responsibility. When David got off track and dropped his spiritual defenses, he fell into sexual sin. For a season, he tried to conceal his transgression by lying, but Nathan confronted him with the words, "You are the man!" David had been found out. It's instructive to see the king's response. When full acknowledgment came, he didn't shift blame by saying, "Bathsheba shouldn't have been taking a bath in open view." Instead, he went before the Lord to acknowledge his sin. You can read his thoughts in Psalm 51, the psalm of confession. So thoroughly did he acknowledge his sin and assume full responsibility, he used three words to describe it: "According to your great compassion blot out my transgressions. Wash away all my iniquity and cleanse me from my sin" (Psalm 51:1b-2).

Note the use of three words: *transgressions*, *iniquity*, and *sin*. There was no blame-shifting, no rationalization, no hot air. There was just open acknowledgment. David had sinned, and he took responsibility for his actions.

I'll never forget Fred sitting across the table from me, tears streaming down his face, saying, "I'm to blame. It's my fault. I assume full responsibility for getting off track." That statement is the foundation for hope. When the prodigal son came home in Luke 15, he simply said, "Father, I have sinned." No shooting the bull, no excuses, just the admission, "I blew it!"

2. Come to the end of yourself.

I've known many men who worked through step one, but then said, "Okay, I admit it—I blew it. It's nothing I can't handle." Really? When the woman with the twelve-year flow of blood came to the end of herself, she was healed. It wasn't until Naaman came to the end of himself and tried things God's way that his leprosy was healed. It wasn't until Jehoshaphat came to the end of himself and said, "Lord, we don't know what to do, but our eyes are on you," that victory came (see 2 Chronicles 20:12). It wasn't until Simon came to the end of himself and launched out into the deep for a catch, that he caught so many fish the nets were breaking.

In 2 Corinthians 1, Paul tells of his exasperating and horrifying experiences of hardship. Because of these experiences he reached a place far beyond his ability to endure, despairing even of life! Then he says something that people today really need to hear: "Indeed, in our hearts we felt the sentence of death. But this happened that we might not rely on ourselves but on God" (2 Corinthians 1:9).

God brought this evangelist to the end of himself, where he could go no further in his own strength. That's when God could reveal His power in Paul's life.

A man was hiking a difficult trail when he slipped on a precipice and fell. Reaching out, he caught hold of a root that kept him from dropping five hundred feet to his death. In desperation, he cried out, "Is anybody up there who can help me?" A voice from heaven said, "I can help you." "Oh, God, it's you. I'll do anything you ask. Just name it." God responded in a thundering voice, *"Let go."* The man paused a moment, looked around, then said, "Is there anybody else up there who can help me?" In reality, the man was only three feet from a ledge that would have saved his life, yet he refused to let go. He wouldn't come to the end of himself.

I love the words of Ian Thomas: "Lord, I can't, but You never said I could. You can, and you always said You would."

3. Find a trusted friend to be your confidant.

Everyone needs another with whom he or she may sit in utmost confidence and make acknowledgment. We each must find someone—a pastor, a Sunday school teacher, a Christian neighbor, a relative who knows the Lord—to whom we pour out our hearts. The Bible says, "Therefore confess your sins to each other and pray for each other so that you may be healed" (James 5:16).

David had Jonathan, Paul had Timothy, Barnabas had Mark. You, too, need that person in your life with whom you may share your pain, your sin, your failures, your weaknesses, your victories, and your dreams. Make sure he is an individual who loves you unconditionally. Make sure he can keep confidences. Make sure he is willing to hold your feet to the fire and is willing to ask you the hard questions. Make sure he's willing to take the time required to be honest with you in a positive way. Make sure he's walking in victory (not perfection) and is strong enough to be your mentor on occasion.

14

4. Humble yourself before God, your spouse, and your friends.

No, it isn't easy, but humbling yourself is a biblical mandate: "Humble yourselves, therefore, under God's mighty hand, that he may lift you up in due time" (1 Peter 5:6).

Notice, the Bible doesn't say that God will humble you, but that you are to humble yourself. What does it mean to humble yourself? It means to get a right assessment of yourself, then openly admit it to those for whom it will make a difference. Men in our culture struggle with "machoism." Impressions are all important. I've talked with many men who've gotten off track in their walks with the Lord. Most of them say, "Well, I struggle from time to time, but over all I'm doing pretty well." What they are really saying is, "I'm in deep yogurt, but I'll never let you know it, or you'll think less of me."

It wasn't until the prodigal son said, "Father, I have sinned" that he was on the road to wholeness. There were many things he could have said. He could have claimed, "I've made a slight tactical error in judgment, but don't worry, it's not a problem at all." He could have argued, "The way you raised me caused me to make self-destructive choices." There is something inside every person that wants to prevent acknowledging failure. Instead, he humbled himself before his father.

I remember the time my new bride and I were driving the 130-mile, one-way trip to our student ministry. In the middle of western Oklahoma, our '53 Chevy lost all its power. It was totally dead. Stopped. Silent. I immediately thought, "I can't let my wife know I know nothing about cars, or I'll be less than a knight in shinning armor in her eyes." So I got out of the car and lifted the hood, not knowing the distributor from the alternator, but pretending to know it all. I went to the side of the car and told her to lock her doors while I went up the road to a farmer's house to borrow some tools. I figured it would give me more time to figure out what to do.

About thirty steps up the road, I heard the engine behind

me start up effortlessly. I turned just in time to see my wife close the hood and wipe her hands. Shrugging her shoulders, she smiled and said, "It was only a loose battery cable." She knew I knew nothing about cars. We had a laugh about it later, but at the time I considered it no laughing matter. Because I didn't humble myself, I was humbled by my wife. In retrospect, I needed that. It takes a real humbling of ourselves to be able to acknowledge that our lives are off track and we need to be changed.

5. Decide to make a definite change.

This is where the hard part begins. An old Chinese proverb says, "He who would walk around the world, must first step off his own porch." If you want to get your life back on track, you must decide to change it.

The essence of repentance lies in turning around. The Greek word for repentance literally means "about face"—to suddenly realize you're going the wrong way, then turn and move in another direction. If you're driving south on the freeway, then find out the town you're trying to reach is in Canada, you have to turn around and drive in the opposite direction. Merely acknowledging the problem isn't enough, you need to do something about it. No one can do it for you. You must do it yourself. You must take the initiative. If your desire to get your life back on track isn't there, the rest of this book is not for you.

When asked, "What did you do when you determined that you wanted to build a theme park?" Walt Disney answered, "I got up, left my office, and visited bank after bank to see who would loan me the money. The first week, no bank I visited would loan me the money, but the second week I found a bank that finally would." Disneyland and Disney World wouldn't exist today had Walt Disney not done something to get the ball rolling. The same is true of your life. Unless you are willing to repent of your sin and make definite changes to your life, that track you left will be void of your presence.

Have you gotten off track? Acknowledgment comes first. You can't skip it or try to circumvent it or cover it up. Half your battle in getting back on track is in acknowledging what has happened. Healing begins when we acknowledge we're sick, wisdom comes when we acknowledge we're ignorant, and fullness comes when we acknowledge we're empty. Spiritual victory comes when we acknowledge we are completely off track and need to get back on. The following prayer is a good way to begin the process of getting back to where God wants you to be.

Lord, I'm on the wrong road. I took the wrong bus, bought the wrong ticket, made the wrong turn, got off in the wrong place, said the wrong things, followed the wrong example, listened to the wrong people, chose the wrong activities, aimed at the wrong target, pulled the wrong trigger, dreamed the wrong dreams, paid the wrong price, and ended up at the wrong destination.

I hereby acknowledge that apart from you, Lord, I am nothing. I confess my need of your direction, your forgiveness, your power, and your motivation to get me moving again. Put me back on track, Lord, and keep my wheels tightly attached. Amen.

Getting Back on Track

What makes you feel your life has gone off the track?

What changes need to be made in your life?

Have you assumed full responsibility for your life?

Do you have a trusted friend who could be your confidant?

What do you need to acknowledge before God? Before your spouse? Before your friends?

Chapter Two

Getting Back on Track Through Quiet Time

USUALLY PEOPLE WHO COMPLAIN about their lives having gotten off track are not spending time with God on a daily basis. Other than a quick prayer at the dinner table, they never seem to be able to find the time to talk with God. It's good to pray with your family at meals, but nothing can substitute for your quiet time, that special time you spend daily in the Word and in prayer and meditation. None of us can ever get back on track until we acknowledge and change this neglected area. Surveys reveal that only 11 percent of Christian men have a quiet time on a consistent basis. Unthinkable! If you want to get your life on track, you must determine you will spend time with the Lord each day. You probably think you can't afford the time it takes to pray and read the Bible every day, but the truth is you can't afford not to.

There are sinister "quiet time robbers" out there that will do their best to steal that necessary time from you. One of them is sleep. It's hard to get up a half-hour earlier in the morning for this all important time. The best way to avoid that robber is to go to bed earlier. For some reason, Americans think they have to watch the late-night news, but this often puts them to bed at midnight. The fact is, if you read the paper each day and catch the headlines on the radio, you'll probably be just as informed. Get to bed earlier and you'll find it easier to get up and spend time with the Lord. (The lack of television's influence will no doubt make you sleep easier, too!)

Your mornings probably consist of shower time, exercise time, breakfast time, dressing time, and commute time—and no room for quiet time with the Lord. Then, after work, you somehow must make time for dinner, paperwork, shuttling the kids, a meeting at church, that extra project that needs your attention, and the TV program you've been wanting to watch. Our busy lifestyles rob us of the time we need to spend with the Lord.

Another time robber is the tyranny of the urgent. We believe there are things we must accomplish, so we go to work earlier than usual or make several stops throughout the day to complete everything on our to-do list. There are so many urgent things needing our attention that we never get around to the thing that matters most—needed time with God; time when He slows us down for a moment to focus on Him.

Then there is the procrastination robber. This robber whispers in your ear, "You're running late today, so you can have your quiet time tonight when you get home." But by the time you return home you're wiped out mentally and emotionally. You tell yourself, "I'll get my Bible out before I go to bed," but you inevitably fall asleep in your chair, stumble groggily to your bed, and another day has gone by without time alone with God. Your intentions are noble, but unrealistic.

I became deeply convicted about my own quiet time years ago when I read these words in the first chapter of Mark: "Very early in the morning, while it was still dark, Jesus got up, left the house and went off to a solitary place, where he prayed" (v. 35). Notice the sequence of events as Jesus becomes our model for a quiet time.

Notice that it was "very early in the morning." (That lets out most of us!) Jesus sensed an appropriate time to confirm God's presence and plan in His life: early in the morning. I think that's a good model. First, your mind is fresh. Problems haven't tracked across it yet to muddy up your concentration. Second, you aren't worn out mentally, physically, or emotionally from the events of the day. Third, it makes a definite spot in your schedule when you know you'll be with the Lord. To plan your quiet time for the evening hours is risky because of unscheduled interruptions. Finally, it starts your day with the Lord and enables everything that comes later to flow through the sieve of Scripture. It makes a difference whether God's Word falls on a tired and weary mind or whether it falls on a fresh, focused mind. That's the early morning advantage.

Also, don't miss the fact that *Jesus got up!* Like it or not, it's necessary to get out of bed. Don't lie there. Don't hit the snooze alarm and go back to sleep. Don't tell yourself, "I need fifteen minutes more sleep today." The truth is, you need time with God more than you need anything else, including breakfast. You may be saying, "But I'm not a morning person!" I fully realize that many people by inclination don't get their motors revved up until later in the day, but my response is, "Become a morning person for Jesus." It will be worth it.

"He left the house and went off to a solitary place." Notice that Jesus went to a private place, a quiet place not inhabited by others. In other words, He got alone. He shut out all the distractions, the noise, and the normal flow of human life so that He could hear God. Find your own place to be alone with God. If you have to get out of your house to find a quiet place, do so.

21

But find a place where it is just you and the Lord.

"He prayed." Jesus made contact with His Father. If the Lord, who is divine, felt the need to have a daily quiet time early in the morning, how much more should we clear time for the same. Learn to talk with God in prayer and spend some time listening to Him, too. Most women I meet seem completely able to have this kind of conversation with the Lord, but many Christian men struggle with the concept of conversing with God.

Since most men I know think in sequential, organized, and outlined ways, let's examine what goes into an effective quiet time. I fully respect your creativity and individuality. You may already have your own system and you're happy with it. If so, skip this section. But, if you don't, or you would like some "fresh oil," hang on and keep reading.

1. Determine the necessity of a quiet time.

The concept of a quiet time has to move from just a good and helpful thing to do, to an *absolute necessity* in your life. We must be thoroughly convinced that we will never get back on track until we get back in touch with God. I have a long list of "good" things I need to be doing, but a quiet time doesn't qualify as just a "good" thing—it's an absolute essential if I'm going to be a man of God.

2. Determine the time of your quiet time.

I'm not suggesting you become a slave of the clock with the same regimen every morning. But if you can say, "Every morning at 6:15 I have my quiet time," people know not to bother you during that time. It's also a good discipline for you. I know a man who lives by his watch so closely that for the last twenty-five years he has eaten breakfast at exactly 7:15 every morning. We need to be as devoted in our time alone with God as we are to our time at work.

3. Determine the place of your quiet time.

I have a definite room in my house where I go every morning at 6:00 A.M. It's my quiet place, my trusting place. I meet God there. I know when I walk into that room at that time, the Lord is already there, waiting for me. Now I don't mean I'm a slave to that. In the summer I may go out on my deck or sit in my backyard, or in the dead of winter I may go into the living room and build a warm fire. But as a rule, I have a predetermined place to get into God's Word, to kneel, and to seek His face.

4. Determine the form of your quiet time.

I'm not suggesting you always follow a certain method or sequence, but I have found that if a person knows what to do first and what to follow that with, he won't waste a lot of time trying to figure out what to do in his quiet time. I've found several steps help me greatly.

Close your eyes, and take about one minute to simply practice the presence of God (see Psalm 46:10). Affirm His presence, perhaps even speak to Him. "Lord, I know you're here, and I long for you to speak to me."

Follow affirmation of God's presence with Bible reading. George Mueller said he always read God's Word before praying, because that way he always had something new for which to praise God! I have found it helpful to read both an Old Testament portion (often a chapter from Proverbs or Psalms) and a New Testament passage. As I read, I ask myself: "Is there a command here to obey? Is there a warning to heed? Is the Lord revealing to me a weakness in my life?"

I've also found it helpful to write out any questions that come to my mind. For example, Romans 12:1 says, "Therefore, I urge you, brothers, in view of God's mercy, to offer your bodies as living sacrifices, holy and pleasing to God—this is your spiritual act of worship." This rich verse proposes all sorts of questions. You might ask, "What does Paul urge me to do with my body? Offer it as a living sacrifice." When you finish a book, you'll have hundreds of didactic questions you can use as a Bible study for others some day. In addition, you will remember what you have read much better if you interact by asking and answering questions. This helps me remember throughout the day what I read in the morning.

Next, spend some time memorizing Scripture. I find it helpful to take five or ten minutes after my Old and New Testament reading to work on memorization. I memorize chapters, not just individual verses. As I am writing this, I'm memorizing Romans 12. It doesn't matter how long it takes you, the point is to hide part of God's Word in your heart daily. I have found some chapters are exceptionally helpful in my Christian walk, and I encourage you to memorize Romans 8, 1 Corinthians 13, 2 Corinthians 4, Galatians 5 and 6, Ephesians 4, Philippians 2, Colossians 3, and the entire book of James.

Finally, pray. Spend some time conversing with God. There is no magic number of minutes. You may start off praying for only five minutes, and eventually pray for an hour. Remember, there is only so much time you have in the morning, so gauge your time. Most people find ten to twenty minutes of prayer each morning comfortable. You may need more—and if you have the time for more, take it!

A good pattern for prayer time is this: thanksgiving, praise and worship, confession, petition (prayer for others), and claiming (letting God know you affirm that He will answer).

Develop a "thank list," enumerating daily all that you're truly thankful for: home, family, spouse, church, health, job, whatever! Don't skip this vital part. Spend a little time adoring God, worshipping Him, and lifting Him up. You may want to sing to Him a hymn, a praise chorus, or even a "new song" (see Psalm 96:1). Create your own song, expressing your feelings to the Lord: "O Lord, I praise you, lift you up, adore you, exalt you, and bless your holy name. Thank you for saving me, being with me, keeping me, and empowering me. Your mercy is great, your power is wonderful, and your love is beyond description. I love you Lord with all my heart." Worship the Lord and give Him the glory due His name.

First John 1:9 tells us to confess our sins to God. This needs to be a very private time of repentance, confession, and contrition. Many people have found it beneficial to lie face down on the floor as a symbol of humbling themselves before the Lord. When you're through confessing your own sins and weaknesses to Him, thank Him for His forgiveness, made possible by the blood of Christ. Bask in that forgiveness for a moment and worship Him.

I have organized how I've chosen to pray for others daily. Every day I pray for my spouse, my children, and my personal witness, and then each day I have special things for which I pray. You may want to do the same. The following prayer suggestions are taken from my personal list.

Monday: Pray for leaders, the president, senators, the governor, the mayor, and people in elected office.

Tuesday: Pray for people you know who are outside of Christ. I keep a list of these, so their names are always with me.

Wednesday: Pray for others' special needs of which you are aware: their problems, marriages, illnesses, work-related issues.

Thursday: Pray for the missionaries your church supports.

Friday: Pray for your pastor and church staff, church leaders, Sunday school class or church group, and the things your church is trying to do.

Saturday: Pray for the areas of your life that need special attention, such as discipline, integrity, relationships, and the things heavy on your heart.

Sunday: On this day, pray for the services of your church, people who teach, usher, serve in other ways, and especially your pastor as he preaches.

I've found this daily prayer time to be refreshing and invigorating. My list enables me to remember all the important issues in my life that require God's attention. Whatever you do, keep a written list and have a place to write in the day God answers your prayer.

Remember, no one can structure prayer for someone else. Prayer, in the words of one pastor, is "laying hold of God." Prayer is to our spirits what breathing is to our lungs. It is not just a good thing to do, it's an *essential* thing. A good definition of prayer is this: "Prayer is finding out what God wants from us." God is not some sanctified genie in a bottle that we rub to get our magic wishes. Prayer is not an attempt to wrench from an unwilling God what He doesn't want to give. Rather, prayer opens the way for God to release what He wants in our lives, but hasn't released, because we haven't prayed.

Also, prayer is conversation between two people who love each other—you and God. It is never meant to be a one-sided conversation, but rather a dialogue in which you speak to Him, and allow sufficient time for Him to speak to you. You may not hear an audible voice, but you can receive in your spirit His impressions. Once you open your heart, God will have no problem finding a way to communicate His will to you. He is not limited, nor is He trying to hide His will from you.

How long does a quiet time take? That's hard to answer, because it is different for each person. Some have found that at least thirty minutes is needed to do it justice; others devote up to one hour. You need to find what is best for your own walk with God, then become consistent in your daily quiet time. Keep some things in mind: First, you probably won't have a spiritual high every day during your quiet time. Some days will stand out beyond others, but *all are helpful*, regardless of how you feel. Second, remember that it's easy to become legalistic about your quiet time and become too structured. Try to avoid that. While you do need form and substance, be flexible, and even more importantly, be faithful. I'm often asked, "Am I ruined if I miss a day of quiet time now and then?" My stock answer is this: You may miss taking a shower one morning and probably no one will notice. If you miss two days, *you* will notice. If you miss more than two days, *others* will definitely notice! A quiet time is very similar. If you miss one day, though it isn't good, you probably won't notice much. If you miss a couple of days, you'll notice. If you miss more than a couple of days, believe me, you and others will really notice!

A third thing to remember is that many things will come along to distract you from your time alone with God. Resist them with all you have, because every day you miss your quiet time, Satan gains ground in your life. I see these times as "putting on the whole armor of God" for your day. Even one day missed can leave you defenseless against the onslaughts of Satan. Since your quiet time is the best place for you to "suit up" with that armor, to miss your opportunity to put it on can invite disaster.

To keep your quiet time from becoming too predictable, occasionally change the order. Pray first some mornings, then get into God's Word. Or perhaps spend the first ten minutes going over your memory verses, then pray. It will keep your quiet time from becoming stale.

If you want to get your life back on track, don't even think of trying to accomplish it without establishing your time alone with God. It is an essential step to finding your way back.

Getting Back on Track

How often do you have a quiet time?

How often would you like to have a quiet time?

What time is best for your quiet time?

Where is the best place for your quiet time?

What would you like to do in your quiet time?

Create a simple schedule for your quiet time, then ask a friend to help keep you accountable.

Chapter Three

Getting Back on Track Through Recommitment to Marriage

AL HAD ATTENDED ONE OF OUR men's discipleship series. Having been a believer for only a year, he was hungry for growth. At the end of the series, Al was doing well. He and his wife were closer than ever before. He was doing things with his family, ushering at the church, going to men's functions, making progress in his quiet time, and had even become involved in an accountability group. Unfortunately, from that spiritual high he started a long, slow slide.

The sequential descent of his spiritual fervor, in retrospect, went like this: First, his quiet time went by the way. Next, he stopped his involvement in his accountability group. Third, he quit going to men's functions. Fourth, his church attendance became inconsistent. Then friction with his wife developed. Later, he started social drinking again, and his temper flared more often.

After all this was in full force, I sat across from him at lunch. He was morose, and I had to virtually pull out of him every fact. He finally said, "I fell off the train somewhere, and I seem to be lost. I don't know what to do." Al's transparent confession is the story of many people. We are prone to take the first or second detour we find in our Christian walk. We seem to have a great propensity to veer; perhaps men more than women.

For almost two hours, Al retraced his downward spiral, which was greatly enhanced by his departure from reading and applying God's Word on a daily basis and his absence of time in the prayer closet. The pulling out of those two simple pins tumbled his whole life into a horrible free-fall that was ruining his health, eroding his marriage to Peggy, and damaging his family. We were at lunch because the night before his wife had suggested they get a legal separation. This was like a jolt of electricity and precipitated his phone call to me. Al was exploding over the slightest things with his wife. He was verbally abusive to her, and even began personal accusations that were totally unfounded. She was a basically quiet woman, very compliant, very supportive of Al for fifteen years, but now she had had it, and wanted out just to sustain her sanity and the sanity of their two children. The sour marriage was dragging everything down. When things aren't right between husband and wife, nothing else is right, whether it be your work, your health, your outlook on life, or your spiritual walk.

Al knew the first thing he had to do to get back on track was reconcile with Peggy, and he didn't have much time to do it. But I'm glad to say that in his case, there was heartfelt repentance, radical change, and fortunately, he got his life back on the right track. To this day he continues to make progress.

Part of getting back on track is rebuilding your relationship and commitment to your spouse. Husband or wife, if your life is off track you are going to have to swallow your pride and recommit to your partner. How do you do that? It's done through the following steps:

- Repentance
- Promises and performance
- Change of personal schedule
- Re-romancing your marriage

Let's begin with repentance. We've been talking about Al, so I'll walk you through his steps with his wife as part of the whole procedure of getting back on track. Repentance isn't just an emotional feeling of regret. It begins with regret, but goes much further. Repentance always does something about the regret. At the suggestion of a small group of men, Al went to his wife and began by confessing to her everything he had done to hurt her. He apologized and took responsibility for the verbal abuse, even to the point of recounting what he had said to her over and over. He renounced those things, and told her he was deeply convicted about them. After that, he asked her to commit to him that she would say something to him if he ever got close to that language again. He also apologized for all the time he spent away from her on purpose. He acknowledged to her that he had rejected her sexually, had used her sexually, and had deliberately lied to her on more than one occasion. Though he had not been sexually unfaithful to her, Al even went so far as to confess that because he was spiritually out of touch with God, he had lived as if he had no wife. I find that a significant confession, since many people experiencing trouble in their marriages begin to live as if they are not really married. That's a blatant violation of God's command that married

31

couples become one, and it reveals the connection between marital health and spiritual health. Al repented of his sin to his wife, the first step in recommitting to his marriage.

The second step is what I call "promises and performance." Al made a commitment to Peggy that, apart from the discipleship group he was entering, he would be home with her every night, unless there was a business emergency. Furthermore, he asked her to help him keep his new commitments, something he had never done in their marriage. Al was much like most men; self-sufficient, self-contained, and selfish. If you need to recommit to your marriage, don't just make promises to your wife or husband. Ask him or her to help you keep your promises. That is like planting seeds of belief, which will grow into a harvest of trust.

The next step for Al was to change his personal schedule to reflect his recommitment to his marriage. He used to spend four or five hours on Saturday mornings playing golf with the guys. Peggy was not included. He also would spend up to three nights a week in a wood-working shop, which was his hobby. It was a costly hobby, because it consistently took him away from his wife in the evenings until way past bed time. Al talked to his wife and changed his schedule. He confined his Saturday golfing to once per month, and began to lose interest in his wood-working once he realized he was using it as an excuse to be away from her. While he might putter around his shop two or three nights per month, it no longer demanded his time. He scheduled Thursday nights as a weekly date with her. Their dates varied from going out to dinner, going to a movie, bowling, or driving into the mountains. He also penciled in an overnight rendezvous with her about every two months. Al's new schedule revealed his commitment to his wife.

Al did something else that was very important. He began romancing his wife. Following the example of another man in the church, Al was inspired to do the following: Send flowers to her for special events. Call her at least twice a day from work. Leave occasional short love notes where she would find them during the day. Buy her occasional gifts on days that were not special days. Kiss her hello and goodbye. Compliment the way she looked.

I know, I know, some of you might be thinking, *That's a little childish, isn't it?* No, it isn't childish, it's romantic. It's manly. It's what God had in mind, I believe, when He tells us in Ephesians 5:25 to love our wives as Christ loved the church. Every man needs to re-evaluate periodically how he is measuring up to that biblical standard. I've found that for me, the following list of questions not only helps me get back on track, but helps me stay on track.

1. Am I attentive to my wife's needs?
2. Do I inquire about her world and how she's doing?
3. Do I *listen* to my wife, or do I just hear her talking?
4. Am I considerate of her opinions and feelings?
5. Do I really believe she is "bone of my bone and flesh of my flesh"?
6. Do I pray for her *daily?* Does she know that?
7. Am I sensitive to the times she doesn't want sex? Am I willing to lovingly wait?
8. Do I attempt to understand how she is feeling?
9. Do I attempt to avoid a critical spirit with her?
10. Do I encourage her ventures?
11. Am I investing enough time to just be with her?
12. Am I willing to occasionally do things with her that she likes even if I don't enjoy them?
13. Do I seek to build her up with my speech instead of tear her down?
14. Am I living with her so that she feels loved and appreciated?
15. Is it clear I am her spiritual leader?
16. Do I initiate prayer, reading God's Word, and going to church?

17. Am I doing my part with her in the discipline of the children?
18. Can she count on me to take the lead in our marriage and make decisions?
19. Am I willing to compromise with her at times in areas that won't violate principle?
20. Does she know I seek to protect her as much as possible from harsh things?
21. Am I willing to rearrange my schedule for her sake?
22. Does she know where she stands in my list of priorities— that next to Jesus Christ she is number one in my life?
23. Is she able to see growth in my spiritual life?

These questions are only a start. You may want to make your own list. I encourage you to read Ephesians 5, Colossians 3, and 1 Peter 3:7 before making your list, so that you have the encouragement of God's Word fresh in your mind. The Bible teaches that you have become one flesh with your wife. This doesn't mean that you give a 50 percent effort to match her 50 percent effort. It means you have blended your love and life together by commitment to the marriage covenant, and are giving 100 percent to make her happy. It means you are one in a very unique way; a way only God can put together. Scripture puts it this way: "For this reason a man will leave his father and mother and be united to his wife, and the two will become one flesh" (Matthew 19:5).

Of course, in that passage Jesus is quoting what His Father had said in Genesis 2:24 when God inaugurated marriage. That "one flesh" relationship defies a simple description:

One flesh means I am one in purity,
   One in purpose,
      One in mind,
         One in emotion,
            And one in sexual union with my spouse.

Of course, it doesn't mean we lose our God-given individuality and uniqueness, but that we have deferred all rights to the one with whom we are one. Paul drove this point home in 1 Corinthians 6:16, when he asked, "Do you not know that he who unites himself with a prostitute is one with her in body?" In other words, Paul is saying marriage is so precious that the sexual union makes you like one person. That's why adultery is so devastating. It violates the one-flesh relationship. It severely wounds and sometimes irreparably damages a marriage.

I believe most men get off track in their marriages because after the first few months or years they begin to take their wives for granted. As long as she meets his sexual needs and keeps the house somewhat clean, he's happy. Most men really don't grasp the teaching for husbands found in Ephesians 5. Between verses 25 and 31, Paul describes the kind of love we are to have for our wives. If we are going to get "back on track" in our marriages, understanding this is an absolute must.

1. The love a husband has for his wife is a divine love.

"Husbands, love your wives, just as Christ loved the church" (Ephesians 5:25). Since we men aren't "divine" in the sense that Christ is divine, we cannot pull that off without reliance on the Lord. Christ loved the Church enough to provide for it, empower it, and die for it. We're called to love our wives in the same way. The Church was the top priority of Christ. Your wife has to become your top priority, so that she knows apart from Christ she is the most important and necessary person in your life.

2. The love a husband has for his wife is a cleansing love.

Ephesians 5:26 tells me that Christ loved the Church so much He was willing to cleanse her. He wants a spotless bride. How does that apply to me? If I love my wife with the biblical love with which I am commanded, my love must be a cleansing love. Part of my role is to make and keep her pure. Now, of course, we all know that Christ has positionally made your wife pure by dying on the cross. But, there is a sense in which God has called me as a husband to "purify" my wife by being pure myself, by keeping sexual impurity and pornography out of my life, and to see to it that she is protected with a covering of purity. This means I won't demand she go to a sexually explicit movie, nor will I demand that she do unnatural things for me to be aroused. I'm called to love her with a cleansing love.

Paul goes on to say, "And to present her to himself as a radiant church, without stain or wrinkle or any other blemish, but holy and blameless" (Ephesians 5:27). I am to be pure, and I am to influence her life with purity.

3. The love a husband has for his wife is a nourishing love.

Paul says, "In the same way, husbands ought to love their wives as their own bodies. He who loves his wife loves himself. After all, no one ever hated his own body, but he feeds and cares for it" (Ephesians 5:28-29). When I met with Al over breakfast that morning, I asked him, "Are you feeding your wife?" His response was altogether wrong: "Well, have you seen her lately? She's put on a lot of weight." He missed my point completely. I wasn't talking about physical food for the body, but spiritual feeding for her soul. Most men avoid this verse, because they think they have to have a doctorate in theology to spiritually feed their wives. Not so. That verse simply means we are to take the initiative to openly share with her what God's Word means to us. We are to take the initiative to pray. We are to take the initiative to sign up for seminars and conferences that will help our relationships. Something as simple as saying, "Honey, I was reading Mark 4 this morning. Let me share something I never saw before" can make a significant difference in nourishing your wife's spiritual life. Something that simple can feed your wife's spiritual hunger and can establish you as the spiritual leader in your home.

4. The husband's love for his wife is a caring love.

Notice how Paul reminds us in Ephesians 4:29 that Christ "cares" for His church. Earlier, Paul had said that we really take pride and time to "care" for our own bodies. We bathe, comb our hair, brush our teeth, and shave each day. It's a priority for us. Do we care the same way for our wives? Does your wife have difficulty knowing where she stands in your order of priorities? Does she know that apart from Christ, she is number one? Does she feel appreciated, admired, loved, and valued? I've learned that wives can live without most anything except priority. They have to know that to you, they count, they matter, and they're important.

Is it easy loving your wife as Christ loves the Church? No, it's one of the toughest things we have to do as men. But is it necessary? Yes! You will not always completely understand your wife, but you are to always love her. Someone has said, "The reason men don't understand women is that men were taking a nap when God created them!" There is probably a lot of truth to that statement. But if you seek to understand your wife, listen to her, and make her a priority, you can learn once again to love her just as Christ loved the church.

Wives, I spent most of this chapter speaking to your husbands, because I believe that if a marriage is going to be successful it will be because the man has decided to love you as Jesus Christ loves the Church. Are you needing to get back on track? Have you drifted slowly away from the closeness you once had to the Lord? Are you living a secular life yet want to go back to a spiritual life? Don't leave your marriage out of your changes. If your marriage is in shambles, you will never be able to get back to being a fully committed disciple of Jesus Christ.

Lord, thank you for my wife, for her patience, her love, her devotion, and her willingness to hang in there until I came around. I hereby recommit myself to her, to our wedding vows, to my role as a husband, to loving her as you loved the church, to tenderness, to showing attention, to leading her spiritually, to doing my part in

37

making our marriage the most wonderful human relationship in all the world. I confess I cannot love her as she was created to be loved by me without your power, your direction, and your intervention. I rededicate my life right now to being a man of God in my marriage. Amen.

Getting Back on Track

What is one thing you could do to show your spouse she/he is your top priority?

Make a list of three things you could do to build the romance of your marriage.

What can you do to build the spiritual life of your spouse?

Husbands, does your wife feel protected?

Wives, does your husband feel served?

Tell your spouse you love her/him, then find a way to show it.

Chapter Four

Getting Back on Track Through Fellowship

I ONCE HEARD ABOUT A LITTLE BOY who fell out of his bed. His mom rushed into his room after hearing the thud and asked him what happened. He responded: "I guess I fell out too close to where I got in." Has that happened to you? Many believers fall out too close to where they got in, and the reason is a lack of fellowship.

Years ago when I took my family of five on a picnic, the kids were playing ball while I was in the midst of cooking hamburgers on a grill. The coals were glowing red. An errant throw hit the portable grill and a couple of coals spilled out on the ground. Because I had plenty of coals going, I decided to leave them where they were. In only a few minutes those two coals cooled to a dark gray, while the coals in the grill continued to glow with intense heat.

Later I thought about those coals and compared them with people. Remove Christians from close fellowship with other believers, and they grow cold, lifeless, and unable to "cook" anything. I believe this is one of the primary reasons Jesus established the Church. It was not just to be a strike-force against the army of Satan, but a haven of fellowship where believers could be bonded, loved, cared for, edified, and encouraged. Christian men may *appear* to be self-sufficient, rugged individualists, but the fact of the matter is we really do need each other. We were created to be social creatures. No man is an island. There is no individual, regardless of his personality, who doesn't need others with whom he can relate.

I was privileged to share Christ with a man who was very shy. After several encounters, Bill finally came to Christ. His life changed. He joined a men's prayer breakfast that met regularly, he and his wife later joined a week-night small group Bible study, and though he didn't make friends easily, he did meet some guys he knew on a first-name basis. Bill was growing, but as Satan would have it, he started missing a Sunday here and there, then more consistently, until he was attending church only about once a month. He was hit and miss with his prayer group, and he and his wife dropped out of their small group, despite the pleadings of the others in the group. One of our pastors finally had lunch with him. After a long conversation, Bill admitted that it all began when he withdrew from other men, crawling back into his shell. He needed the prod, and thanks to persistence on the part of his prayer group, they got Bill back into fellowship. His life blossomed, and he's faithful to this day. What happened to Bill happens to many people. Their train falls off the track due to lack of fellowship.

Some of us get nervous when someone starts talking about fellowship between men. Women have no problem "bonding" with other women. Put five women in a room who have never met each other, and within an hour, they are sharing on a deep level with one another. Put five men in a room who have never met each other, and within an hour they have gotten no deeper than what they do for a living, sports scores, and the latest draft choices.

It seems to take months, in some cases years, before a male will share with another male his struggles in life, whether it's his marriage, work, or personal existence as a man. We've heard all the descriptions: Men are macho. Men are self-reliant. Real men don't touch other men, unless it's an occasional high-five. Men don't have feelings, aren't easily moved in their emotions, and tend to think in terms of goals, numbers, figures, quotas, and outcomes. Many men believe that unless they are a John Wayne, James Bond, or Arnold Schwarzenegger, they are effeminate. They are competitive in nature with one another, whether it be in business, sports, or money, so that they seldom see another male as someone with whom to develop deep camaraderie. Many men are suspicious of other men. A man's need for friends is an urgent need. If you were to die, would your wife have a problem making a list of six close friends to carry your casket? Think about it. Who would she ask? Are you in fellowship with other guys?

Maybe by now you're wondering, "Just what is fellowship?" It's probably an over-used word in our Christian vocabulary, so let me begin by describing what it isn't. It doesn't mean seeing a guy you know at church and saying, "How are you?" so that he responds, "Fine, and you?" You answer by saying, "Fine," then the two of you go your merry way. That may be politeness, but it's not fellowship. Fellowship isn't sitting in a Bible study group with other men, learning Scripture from a teacher. You may never even know the names of the other guys. Fellowship isn't going out for coffee with the guys after a meeting, it isn't attending a men's prayer breakfast, and it isn't showing up for a church work day. All of those things are fine, but not neces-sarily fellowship. Fellowship is never surface conversation.

Then what is fellowship? The Greek word is *koinonia*, and the root of that word has to do with sharing, giving, and receiving. It means participation, or having something in common. For example, in 1 Corinthians, Paul tells us it's something we experience at the Lord's table. "Is not the cup of thanksgiving for which we give thanks a participation in the blood of Christ? And is not the bread that we break a participation in the body of Christ?" (1 Corinthians 10:16).

The word translated "participation" in that verse is *koinonia*. In other places in the New Testament, it is translated "fellowship." It literally means "to share something in common," which is how we came to call that ritual "Communion."

Holy Communion is more than merely eating a small wafer and drinking a cup of grape juice. It is a deep spiritual experience we share with Jesus and He shares with us. In the same way, fellowship is sharing deeply with another person in areas that affect your spirit, not just your mind and body.

Physically, the game of basketball causes men to share their bodies with each other. Sometimes it's a hand across the face, a foot across the ankle, or an elbow across the other guy's arm. That's physical fellowship. Spiritual fellowship goes a bit deeper. It's more than casual guy talk. It's a spiritual bonding and closeness that can best be described as "one-another" ministry. The Bible often talks about meaningful relationships in terms of what we do to and with one another:

We submit to one another (Ephesians 5:21).
We forgive one another (Ephesians 4:32).
We serve one another (Galatians 5:13).
We live in peace with each other (1 Thessalonians 5:13).
We are kind to one another (1 Thessalonians 5:15).
We encourage one another (1 Thessalonians 5:11).
We love one another (John 13:34).
We honor one another (Romans 12:10).
We accept one another (Romans 15:7).

We instruct one another (Romans 15:14).
We confess our sins and pray for one another (James 5:16).

I could go on and on, but that list is enough to convince me that I am to be in a *sharing* relationship with other men, not merely a *surface* relationship. Obviously, we can never participate in another brother's life unless we are willing to spend enough quality time with him for it to come about. I need what other men can give. They need what I uniquely can give. I'm told in Proverbs 27:17, "As iron sharpens iron, so one man sharpens another." Without the context of fellowship, where iron can sharpen iron, we will be dull indeed.

When Jesus chose His disciples, He had a purpose in gathering about Himself a group of men rather than just one person. He wanted to pour His life into those men, but He also desired to simply "be with" them. In Mark 3, it says of their calling, "He appointed twelve—designating them apostles—that they might be with him" (v. 14).

Jesus certainly saw the wisdom of fellowship. He knew that these men could and would do as a group what they could never do by themselves. Perhaps this is why Solomon, in his wisdom, wrote:

> Two are better than one, because they have a good return for their work: If one falls down, his friend can help him up. But pity the man who falls and has no one to help him up! Also, if two lie down together, they will keep warm. But how can one keep warm alone? Though one may be overpowered, two can defend themselves. A cord of three strands is not quickly broken (Ecclesiastes 4:9-12).

The stories of Scripture bear this out. Moses had Aaron, David had Jonathan, Elijah had Elisha, Paul had Timothy, Barnabas had Mark, Jesus had His twelve, and within that dozen were an even more intimate group of three. Who do you have? God places a premium on fellowship. Whether it's another guy, a small group, or even a larger group, fellowship assures us that the following things take place.

Encouragement

Who doesn't need to be encouraged from time to time? You cannot be strengthened and encouraged if you live in a vacuum, uninvolved with other people. Stress is seriously damaging men today as they attempt to balance work, home, church, debt, and the various responsibilities of life. Someone has said we are so busy, we're honking at our own taillights! In the midst of it all, we need an individual or two who will come alongside and put their arms around our shoulders. That's why I have appreciated the recent surge of men's conferences. What a sight to see a stadium full of men with their arms linked together, even if it is for only a few hours.

A good example of encouragement is found in Exodus 17. Moses was weary, having fought the Amalekites. When he stood on the hill with his hands in the air, his team was winning. When his hands came down to his side, his team was losing. He needed strength and encouragement. Aaron and Hur noticed he was growing weary, so they stood on each side of Moses, got under his arms, and held them up for him. The Bible says his hands remained steady until sunset, and the battle was won as Joshua led them to victory. I've often thought we men need to begin a ministry called, "The Fellowship of Arm-Holders." We were not meant to get through this life alone. We need others standing with us.

I thank God for men who, through the years, have put their arms around me, especially during those very low times in my ministry. I'm glad they were there. Their presence and their words brought me encouragement when I needed it most.

Edification

Apart from our mentors and close friends, most of us are left to a system of "self-taught manhood." There is a lot we can teach ourselves by reading, watching others, and listening to tapes, but let's face it, we still need men around us who sharpen us, challenge us, and impart wisdom to us. I'm thankful especially for the older men in my younger years who taught me so much from their overflow of maturity. I've seen men come alive in their knowledge of the Word just by being in a discipleship or accountability group. We need fellowship for edification.

The word "edification" means literally "to build up." That's what fellowship allows us to do. We build others up until they are mature in Christ. We get built up by others so that we are strong. We recognize that we are a part of a strong team that God has pulled together to accomplish His purposes on earth. That's why Paul told the Thessalonians, "Therefore encourage one another and build each other up" (1 Thessalonians 5:11).

Accountability

Years ago when our church was much smaller, we had a motto: "You don't get what you *expect*, you only get what you *inspect*." Every man needs another man who will commit to hold his feet to the fire, ask him the hard questions, and keep him focused when he's tempted to veer. Every woman needs an accountability partner, someone she feels close to and to whom she can share her feelings. I have a great accountability group of six men. I chose them on the basis of one criterion—they aren't afraid to ask me the hard questions. Are you in the Word? Are you investing enough time in your wife? Did you stay pure on your last trip? Did you peruse the pornography on the magazine rack when you were two thousand miles from home? Are you getting proper rest? Are you disciplined in your eating habits? What about your weight? No, I don't like those questions, but I need them. You need them, too! If you want to be in proper fellowship, you need others who care enough to confront you with accountability questions.

Service

Isolation breeds non-involvement. If we aren't in relationship to other Christians, we tend to stop ministering and serving in the body of Christ. I've been told that only 37 percent of men in the average Evangelical church are doing any Christian service. I hope that statistic is wrong, but I fear it's accurate. More women are in service, but even their numbers are dropping as they become involved with careers of their own. Scripture calls us to serve one another and to serve with one another. It's much more exciting to serve with others than to serve alone. I'm told in 1 Peter 4:10 that as I have received my giftedness, I am to use it for the good of the body. When you're out of fellowship, there is no incentive to serve.

Do you want to get back on track? The process starts with acknowledging the problem, it goes on to reestablishing your quiet time, recommitting to your marriage, and it isn't compete without renewing your fellowship to the body of Christ.

How Do I Get Started?

1. Ask a mature Christian to disciple you.

2. Find a group of men or women meeting for Bible study and join them.

3. Find some people who would like to meet once a week for prayer and let it become an accountability group.

4. Get involved in a home fellowship group.

Getting Back on Track

Where do you experience fellowship?

What do you like best about fellowship?

Who do you know that needs your encouragement?

Who encourages you?

If you could choose anyone as an accountability partner, who would you select?

In what service are you involved?

Chapter Five

Getting Back on Track Through Right Priorities

SURELY YOU'VE HEARD ABOUT the man who played golf daily. One day he was on the seventh hole, which ran parallel to the main road. A funeral procession was passing by, so he took off his hat, held it to his chest, and bowed his head until the hearse had passed by. His playing partner said to him, "That was a fine thing to do." The golfer replied, "Yes, and bless her heart, tomorrow we would have been married twenty-five years." Now that is a prime example of a man whose priorities are not in order!

Unless you are Superman, able to juggle all the responsibilities of your life without ever dropping a ball, you have struggled with right priorities. You may even be struggling now. I remember a morning not long ago when I had a 6:00 breakfast meeting, a 7:15 recording session, an 8:30 conference call at my office, a 9:00 staff meeting, I was supposed to have my car in the mechanic's shop for repair by 8:00, and all of this was on the day of the week I set aside for sermon preparation! I felt frazzled, unproductive, and inefficient in everything I did that day. I had obviously scheduled too many things into one small period of time. I was not fit to live with that evening when I came home to my wife. (Just ask her!) Everybody has those days. The key is that if you're going to get your life on track, you have to sort through your priorities.

Part of getting back on track is gaining God's perspective on what is a priority and what isn't. That's not as easy as it sounds. Men are very different from women and have a different sense of priorities. When my wife talks about priorities, she always talks about relationships. When I talk about priorities, I talk about activities. I want to know what's *essential*, *important*, and *desirable*. Men today are bombarded with demands on their time and energy from family, work, friends, neighbors, church, and finances. Because a man's identity is so closely tied to his work, he often finds it very difficult to balance his time between his personal life and his professional life.

Many years ago, I read a little booklet entitled, "The Tyranny of the Urgent." It pointed out how we become enslaved to this tyranny so that there is no room left for planning. The author referred to it as a "preoccupation with the immediacy of the urgent." All you can think about is the immediate need. It is also called, "fire-extinguisher" living, because you are constantly reacting to one crisis after another, trying to put out one fire before another begins. I know a man who carries a large supply of antacids around with him, because in his words, "I get acute indigestion about five to seven times each day while putting out fires." He is no firefighter—he's a unit manager at a large manufacturing firm with about fifteen people working under him. But he feels constant pressure, and he is always on the watch for an upcoming disaster.

A typical male's scale of priorities generally looks like this:

1. Work
2. More work
3. Over-time work
4. Church work
5. Wife, home, and family
6. Hobby
7. House chores
8. Jesus Christ

If we're going to get back on track with our priorities, our list will have to dramatically change. Christ must be first and our wives second. Perhaps our careers will have to be less important and our church work more important. The reason so many of us are trapped in an avalanche of work is because we have bought into the world's premise that "He who dies with the most toys, wins." We spend all our time working ourselves to death so that we can have a bigger house, a better car, nicer things, and a more impressive funeral. Then, when our marriages are falling apart and our children don't know us, we can turn to them and say, "But I did it all for you!" The fact is, the priorities of the world are at war with the priorities of God. And he who dies with the most toys still dies...probably alone and unhappy. That's why one of the things Christians need to add to their list of priorities is something called "short- and long-range planning." You need to make it a priority in your life.

Assessment and Evaluation

The place to begin is at the beginning. What are your priorities right now? The best way to get a handle on your life is to first determine what is running it. I have found that the most productive way to begin making short- and long-range plans is to make an assessment of your life. Take a week, maybe starting this Monday, and write down exactly what you're doing in thirty minute increments. What did you do from 7:00 to 7:30? From 7:30 to 8:00? Don't change your schedule, just record what you are doing in your life now. A chart would look something like this:

Monday	Tuesday	Wednesday	Thursday
5:00_____	_____	_____	_____
5:30_____	_____	_____	_____
6:00_____	_____	_____	_____
6:30_____	_____	_____	_____
7:00_____	_____	_____	_____
7:30_____	_____	_____	_____

(and so on until the time you go to bed at night.)

Write down everything, including your commute to and from work, time spent eating, coffee breaks, watching television, reading the newspaper, shooting the breeze with others—*everything you do*. Don't leave anything out. Then you'll have a handle on where your time goes.

Everyone is given the same amount of time each week: 168 hours. Find out how much of your time is wasted. Find out what you could do in shorter time. Find out what is taking most of your time. It will probably be your work. Most men work about fifty hours per week. Some work a few hours more or less than that, but you'll probably find fifty hours about right. How are you spending your evenings? Take an inventory. You can't make any changes until you first determine what needs to change.

Identify Your Time Robbers

Time robbers come in all shapes and sizes. Most of them come in the form of people who have a way of stealing your time from you—time you could be spending with your family or church. For some people, disorganization in their work wastes a great deal of time. One man recently said to me, "I just got organized at work with a game plan and created almost four hours every week!"

Sometimes, people needlessly take up your time with things that could easily be handled by someone else. It doesn't take you long to identify those people. I've found when they come into my office, I stand up and tell them, "I have four or five minutes right now, how may I help you?" When that time is up, I check my watch and politely say, "I really need to get back to my project right now, but I will do what I can." If the problem isn't solved then, I simply say, "Could we set another time to discuss this?" (By the time that meeting rolls around, the problem has usually taken care of itself or has been solved another way!) Short exchanges in the hallway about weather, sports, politics, or current events are to be expected at work, but when they happen several times each day, they steal precious time from us and prevent us from having our priorities in place.

Television is a time robber. You get almost nothing out of your time with the tube, yet it consumes many people. Be honest about how much time you actually sit glued to the set in seven days—for many people it is a revelation! Reading a newspaper thoroughly can become a serious time-robber. I used to spend almost forty-five minutes daily reading the paper. I would read the sports section from cover to cover, then the editorial page, the international section, the obituaries, the entertainment section, and on and on. Someone convicted me by asking the question, "Are you spending the same amount of time in God's Word that you do reading the daily newspaper?" I was nailed. Now I catch the headlines, scan for sermon illustrations, grab a sports score here and there, then lay it down. Five to ten minutes is all I'll give it anymore. The same thing is true with magazines. There was a time when I was a magazine buff. I used to consistently read three or four major magazines per week. I seldom read any now, not because I wouldn't like to, but because they were robbing two or three hours of my precious time per week, and knocking my priorities out of kilter.

Write Your Priorities in Sequential Order

This is not easy, but it's essential. I can't write your priorities for you, but I can give you some guidelines. Time spent developing your personal relationship with Jesus Christ must be at or near the top. This includes your quiet time, your Bible study, class preparation, and time spent reading the Scriptures with your spouse and family.

Time spent serving and romancing your mate is another high priority, although many men will have to add this to their list. I've always said that next to my commitment to Jesus Christ is my commitment to my wife. This means I have to be proactive in developing a trusting, loving, leading relationship with my wife. I must forever ask the question, "Does she know she stands at the top of my pecking order?" Husbands, if you don't make plans to romance your wife, your marriage will always be a little flat. Wives, if you don't make an effort to serve your husband, there won't be any "zing" to your relationship. Make your partner a priority.

Next comes the rest of your family. Do your children know, for example, that their ball games are a high priority to you? Do they know that your helping them with their homework or going outside to ride bikes with them is important to you? Ask yourself, "Do I spend more time with my children than I do sitting in front of the TV?" How you spend your time reveals your priorities. If you aren't spending time with your family, they realize they are not important to you. Change your priorities so that your family comes ahead of your job and your entertainment.

Of course your work is important. I have to earn a living, therefore at least forty hours of my week will be spent devoted to my job. But never allow the making of money to usurp your health, family, marriage, or personal relationships. Most men have no difficulty listing their jobs as a priority, they simply have a tough time trying to squeeze in anything else. But if your job is your God, then your life is out of balance. A workaholic is a person who believes his personal worth comes not from God, but from his own efforts. That's one of the oldest misconceptions around—it's what led Cain to kill Abel! Don't buy into the world's standards of success and significance. Look at what God says is important and follow His prescription.

Service for Christ and His Church needs to be on your list of priorities. I believe every Christian needs to weave at least two or three hours a week into serving the church, and that doesn't mean simply showing up on Sunday mornings. God established the Church to accomplish His purposes and change the world. As a Christian, you have a responsibility to be part of that task. If you are not fulfilling your part, you are absent without leave. This is "Christianity 101." You have to demonstrate what you believe in your heart by living out your faith. That confirms the fact that you are a disciple of Jesus Christ. But be careful. Many Christians get caught up with eight to fifteen hours per week at church, to the neglect of their families at home. I think that, for some people, it becomes an escape from an unhappy marriage. Make sure you are walking with God, put a priority on strengthening your marriage and family, then decide to serve the Lord through the church.

Everyone needs to spend some time in his or her week for planning purposes. If I don't do this for short- and long-term planning, I'm soon sunk in a morass of "urgent" stuff and I never get around to the "important" things. After all of this, we need to squeeze some time in, on occasion, for recreation or hobbies. This needs to include some kind of physical exercise as well as rest. Our bodies are the temple of the Holy Spirit, and we have stewardship of their care. If we neglect our bodies, we dishonor God by having a shabby temple.

Create a Schedule for Yourself

The best way to get back on track in your priorities is to set yourself up on a fairly disciplined schedule. This isn't bondage to the calendar and the clock, but taking control of your own life. Make no mistake about it, if you don't write out and set your own schedule, someone else will set it for you. Either you will be in charge of your life or someone else will. You certainly don't have to be a slave to that schedule, because obviously there are interruptions during the week. But it's better to aim at something and hit it occasionally than to aim at nothing and hit it every time. It's easier to adjust a schedule when the need arises than to try to create one as you go along.

One warning: You want to be realistic as you weave into that schedule the obvious things such as spending time with your family, commuting to work, eating, sleeping, and the like. I have seen Christians set up written schedules they knew they couldn't live by, but they looked good and impressed others. That is nonsense! If it normally takes you thirty-five minutes to get to work, don't put down on your schedule that you'll get there in twenty. You're setting yourself up for failure. Let your written schedule be an honest and accurate record, then you will be able to see if you are getting out of balance some place. Written schedules help keep your priorities on track. I usually divide my day into three periods; morning, afternoon, and evening. How much time and energy I'm giving to a thing lets me know quickly where it stands on my scale of priorities.

Paul wisely said, "Be very careful, then, how you live—not as unwise, but as wise, making the most of every opportunity" (Ephesians 5:15-16). That doesn't mean to pack into your daily schedule so many activities you can't possibly pull them off. Everyone is given the same amount of time, and we can either accomplish much by making the most of it or we can fritter away that time with non-productive junk. What do you value most? What consumes most of your time, energy, and creativity? Is it your job? I hope not. Workaholics are people who see their jobs as the ultimate idol to bow down to, even to the point of squeezing out the most important things in life: their relationship to Christ and personal support of and commitment to the kingdom of God. Is it the television? If so, you have put your need to be entertained above God's call for your life to reflect His priorities.

When an individual comes to the end of his life, and lies on his deathbed, you will never hear him complain that he didn't spend enough time at the office. No, it's usually that he didn't spend enough time with his family. A vital part of getting back on track is reestablishing priorities. As a fully devoted disciple of Jesus Christ, your list of important things will differ vastly from the man who isn't following Christ. Let your life reflect the priorities of God.

Getting Back on Track

Are you devoting too much time and energy to temporal things?

Are you willing to "take charge" of your time instead of allowing others to write your schedule?

Will you dare to put your Lord and family at the very top of the list?

Are you willing to have another person hold you accountable to your new schedule?

Will you ask God right now (before going to the next chapter), to give you the wisdom to write out your new agenda and priorities?

Chapter Six

Getting Back on Track Through Personal Finances

DARWIN CAME TO CHRIST in his mid-twenties. He had been married at nineteen years old at the insistence of his parents when they discovered his girlfriend was four months pregnant. He and Sue struggled early in their relationship until Darwin, in his immaturity, moved out after four years of marriage.

Darwin worked at an industrial company. His immediate supervisor was a Christian who knew Darwin was very depressed about being unable to keep up his support payments to Sue and their little boy. He invited Darwin to church, and he came. Sue was thrilled as she had become a Christian herself. In only a matter of weeks, Darwin yielded his life to Christ and became deeply involved in the church. He was active in the men's fellowship, ushered during the Sunday services, and played on the church softball team. Soon he became involved in a men's discipleship group in which he grew by leaps and bounds.

Being a stock car racing fan, Darwin began missing church about once a month to attend races. After a while he was skipping church twice a month, and soon he was attending only occasionally to satisfy his wife. Their finances, which greatly improved after he came to Christ, began to be severely tested. Darwin stopped living according to their budget and began to squander his money. He quit ushering, left the men's discipleship group, no longer played softball with the men of the church, and seemed to grow completely disinterested in spiritual things.

The Bible says, "We must pay more careful attention, therefore, to what we have heard so that we do not drift away" (Hebrews 2:1). I don't know anyone who leaps out of fellowship with the Lord; it's a slow, subtle process. Darwin seemed to be drifting away from the Lord, until something dramatic happened. He met a crisis: an illness of one of his children. It was amazing how quickly he called out to God. His old boss came alongside him and began to encourage him, was instrumental in helping him develop a quiet time, and helped Darwin reestablish his relationship with God, his fellow believers, and his family.

In the process of coming back, part of Darwin's struggle lay in the area of personal finances. We reap what we sow, and Darwin had run up a large amount of bills. It was money he had spent on foolish things, and he was deeply in debt. Through the efforts and influence of his boss, Darwin took some strong steps to resume a responsible attitude toward money. Though it took time and discipline, he was able to get back on track in this difficult area.

Most people are not naturally good managers of money. All

of us are selfish and prefer to spend our resources on ourselves. Some of us were never offered any training in the proper use of personal finances. However, a very large part of our lives is taken up with receiving and spending money. Therefore, I want to present some principles of personal finance that will help you in your trek back into fellowship and closeness with the Lord Jesus Christ. Use these principles and steps as a guideline to help you get back on track in your personal finances.

1. Recognize that God owns everything.
The Bible teaches that the Lord is the owner of all things. In Psalm 24:1 it says, "The earth is the LORD's, and everything in it." In Psalm 50:10-12 David also wrote these words, "For every animal of the forest is mine, and the cattle on a thousand hills. I know every bird in the mountains, and the creatures of the field are mine. If I were hungry I would not tell you, for the world is mine, and all that is in it."

This is a very radical principle we are called to embrace. It's the principle that we are not owners, but managers. We simply manage what God releases to us. So strong did Jesus feel about this as a condition of discipleship, He said these words: "Any of you who does not give up everything he has cannot be my disciple" (Luke 14:33). I love the way the Amplified Bible translates that verse: "So then, whoever of you does not forsake—renounce, surrender claim to, give up, say goodbye to all that he has—cannot be My disciple."

You see, it makes a world of difference as to whether we are owners or managers. As owners, we set the agenda; we determine how we use what we have. We decide whether we are going to buy or sell, give or take. But as managers, that decision is not left to us. We are under the headship of the owner. Whatever the owner desires, we must be willing to do. Since God is the owner of all things, we must relinquish any kind of supposed ownership we may have thought we had.

61

2. As managers, we are accountable to the owner.

Jesus told an earth-shaking parable in Matthew 25 that has often been referred to as the parable of the "talents." A talent was a weight representing money and was worth approximately $1,000 dollars. In the parable, Jesus told about a man going on a journey who called his servants and entrusted his property to them. To one he gave five talents, roughly $5,000; to another he gave two talents, and to another one talent. The account in Matthew 25 tells us he gave differing amounts according to the ability of the recipients.

While the master was gone the man who received the $5,000 doubled the investment. The one who had $2,000 also doubled his investment. However, the one who had been given $1,000 had buried his money in the ground so that when his master returned, he gave back exactly what the master had given to him earlier. Jesus commended the two men who had doubled the money that had been left with them, but for the man who had buried his talent and brought back only what he began with, Jesus had disdain. "You should have put my money on deposit with the bankers," the master in Jesus' parable said, "so when I returned I would have received it back with interest." In other words, Jesus wants a return on His investment. He wants us to manage His property with shrewdness and creativity. He doesn't want us to squander, misuse, or abuse what He has entrusted to us. This means, when we receive our paycheck, it is not left up to us alone to decide how to use it. Our agenda comes from God.

In 1 Corinthians 4:1-2 we read, "So then, men ought to regard us as servants of Christ and as those entrusted with the secret things of God. Now it is required that those who have been given a trust must prove faithful." God expects us to prove faithful with what He has entrusted to us, whether it be the gospel, money, or anything else. God is the owner of everything, and we are His managers. As such, we are accountable to the owner for how we use what He has given us. Someone put it like this, "God is concerned with how we earn our money, God is concerned with how we spend our money, God is concerned with how we save our money, and God is concerned with how we give our money." As managers of His resources, it is only fair that the Lord takes an interest in what we do with our money.

3. God wants us to give biblically.

When we talk about getting back on track, a very large portion of returned has to do with our personal responsibility of honoring God. He has not left us in the dark to grope and wonder how we are to give. God has a plan for your finances. If you will order your financial life according to His principles, He has promised to bless.

The best place to start is with the tithe. The Bible says,

> "Bring the whole tithe into the storehouse, that there may be food in my house. Test me in this," says the LORD Almighty, "and see if I will not throw open the floodgates of heaven and pour out so much blessing that you will not have room enough for it. I will prevent pests from devouring your crops, and the vines in your fields will not cast their fruit," says the LORD Almighty (Malachi 3:10-11).

I believe God wants us to begin our giving journey with a tithe; 10 percent of whatever comes to us. In the Old Testament the Jew actually had three tithes he was required by law to give. At the time of Malachi they spoke of only one tithe. The command to tithe is followed with a promise: If you give, God will pour out so much blessing you won't have room for it all. God also promises to prevent anything from destroying your wealth. In those days agriculture was the medium of exchange. The "pests" referred to were locusts and grasshoppers, which invaded the fields of wheat and barley and reduced them to mere stubble. A farmer's profit could be severely reduced by these pests. Those crops represent money. The pests that attack our money these days are inflation and taxes, and I believe God promises to rebuke them for us if we tithe. Now I don't think God is likely to change the inflation rate, or single us out to say we don't have to pay taxes, but what He will do is miraculously provide us enough money so that our resources are not eroded away with these twin devourers. I have seen Him work that way time after time in my own finances.

While the tithe is a wonderful place with which to start, it certainly is not the maximum or the ultimate place. As Christians, we have much more than the Jew had. We have the gift of eternal life. We have the assurance of salvation, the hope of heaven, and the presence of the Holy Spirit in our lives. If the Jew tithed under the Old Covenant and had none of these, it seems to me we need to be going far beyond the tithe in our financial devotion to the Lord. I have suggested to people for years to increase their giving by 1 percent each year. This means if you are tithing 10 percent now, next year give 11 percent. The following year give 12 percent and so on. God certainly will honor that ascending scale.

I have heard many Christians say, "But Pastor, I cannot afford to tithe." If God has promised to prevent pests from devouring your profits, it seems to me you cannot afford not to tithe. Besides, if you have faith enough to believe other parts of Scripture, certainly you ought to have faith enough to believe that God will do what He says in Malachi 3:10-12.

4. We are to believe the promises of God.

This is a very controversial issue, but I believe it needs to be addressed. I certainly do not want to come across as being in favor of the "health and wealth gospel," for I do not believe the Bible teaches that God necessarily wants everyone to be healthy and wealthy. However, God does want us to believe the promises He has made. Throughout both the Old and New

Testaments there seems to be a pattern of giving followed by a promise of God to act in one's life. For example, in Proverbs 3:9-10 it says, "Honor the LORD with your wealth, with the firstfruits of all your crops, then your barns will be filled to overflowing, and your vats will brim over with new wine." Notice the command is to honor the Lord with your wealth. The promise follows that you will experience abundance if you obey. That almost sounds like the promise is predicated upon the obedience of the command.

The same thing is true in Proverbs 11:24-25: "One man gives freely, yet gains even more; another withholds unduly, but comes to poverty. A generous man will prosper; he who refreshes others will himself be refreshed." Notice the result of a man who gives freely. He "gains even more." The promise given to a man who practices generosity is that he will prosper. Solomon is right on target in Ecclesiastes 11:1 when he says, "Cast your bread upon the waters, for after many days you will find it again." The man who gives generously will reap a generous reward.

When we come to the New Testament, the biblical principle of giving is stated clearly by the Lord Jesus in the Sermon on the Mount. "Give, and it will be given to you. A good measure, pressed down, shaken together and running over, will be poured into your lap. For with the measure you use, it will be measured to you" (Luke 6:38). God is trying to get your attention by saying if you will give faithfully, He will return an abundance so you can give even more. This seems to be God's economy plan.

Perhaps the most pointed promise concerning our giving is recorded for us in 2 Corinthians 9:6: "Whoever sows sparingly will also reap sparingly, and whoever sows generously will also reap generously." In verse 8 Paul goes on to share the great promise of those who give generously: "And God is able to make all grace abound to you so that in all things at all times, having all that you need, you will abound in every good work."

65

He also says, in verse 11 of that same chapter, "You will be made rich in every way so that you can be generous on every occasion, and through us your generosity will result in thanksgiving to God." God has promised to enlarge the supply of our seed, predicated upon the fact that we are sowing, or giving generously. This principle has often been referred to as the "Law of the Harvest."

We reap what we sow. If we sow corn, we reap corn. If we sow peas, we reap peas. If we sow onions, we reap onions. It is the law of the harvest that you reap in kind what you sow. But there is also a sense in which we reap in amount what we sow. If you sow in a skimpy way, you will certainly reap a sparing harvest. The same is true in other areas of your life. If you don't sow much encouragement to others, you usually don't get much encouragement from others. If you don't sow much joy to others, you will receive very little joy back from others.

That same principle is true of money. If you sow lavishly, God has a way of giving back lavishly so that you can give even more the next time. I once heard a preacher say, "I shovel in and God shovels out, and He has a bigger shovel." We will never get back on track with our personal finances until we learn to give consistently, lavishly, and in accordance with God's will revealed in Scripture.

5. God wants you to be debt free.

Let me make one thing clear up front—when I talk about debt I am talking about bills you owe that either you cannot pay or that have plunged you into bondage. It is not wrong to have financial obligations to the electric company, the gas company, and the home mortgage company, as long as you are able to pay those obligations. I believe God wants us to work and move toward becoming free of the encumbrance of debt. Owing money is not unbiblical. In fact, a careful reading of Old and New Testament passages dealing with finances reveals there is nothing inherently wrong with owing money. Several

Bible characters borrowed money. There is no hope of owning a home for most Americans apart from a mortgage. However, incurring bills you have no intention of repaying, nor money to repay, certainly is wrong.

Having an ongoing debt that is so exorbitantly high you have little hope of repaying places you in an awkward relationship with the one who holds that mortgage. Perhaps this is why Solomon said, "The rich rule over the poor, and the borrower is servant to the lender" (Proverbs 22:7). That kind of servanthood is not good, nor should it continue. Part of getting back on track is working toward reducing your indebtedness and setting some goals and a timeline to get yourself completely out of debt. Even if your timeline is ten years long, at least you'll have a plan for getting out of debt.

The best place to begin on this project is to develop a budget for you and your family. I have found it very helpful in budgeting to have two columns; one listing all of the fixed obligations and the other the fluctuating expenses. The first column would include rent, utilities, tithe, insurance, and all obligations that are fixed each month. The second column would list things such as entertainment, eating out, clothing, car repairs, and other things that tend to fluctuate but still need to be budgeted. A budget is not meant to enslave you but to be your servant. It causes you to draw some parameters for your spending. It is probably your greatest defense against compulsive spending.

When these five principles are adhered to, you can rest assured you are getting back on track in your personal finances. We need to remember that Jesus said, "For where your treasure is, there will your heart be also." You can tell a lot about where a Christian's priorities are by examining his check stubs. The things to which we devote our money are those which we also devote our energy and commitment.

Below are the ten commandments for personal finances:

1. Thou shalt acknowledge that everything belongs to God.
2. Thou shalt further know that thou art accountable.
3. Thou shalt look at thy possessions as a trust from God.
4. Thou shalt always tithe of thy income, regardless of its size.
5. Thou shalt avoid being a tightwad and a spendthrift.
6. Thou shalt operate thy financial world with a well-crafted budget.
7. Thou shalt be generous to thy wife with thy money.
8. Thou shalt avoid impulse buying.
9. Thou shalt not run up consumer debt with thy credit card.
10. Thou shalt not fall into the trap of loving money and desiring to be wealthy.

Getting Back on Track

Do you live as though "God owns everything"?

Who keeps you accountable to your budget?

What percent of your income do you give away?

What percent would you like to give away?

What promises has God made to you about your finances?

What steps do you need to take to move toward becoming debt-free?

Chapter Seven

Getting Back on Track Through Personal Holiness

TED WAS THIRTY YEARS OLD when he came with his best friend to my office. Ted was tall, very handsome, and very successful in his own business. That day his good looks were blemished by red eyes and a furrowed brow. He had received Christ when he was twenty-one through the ministry of a buddy in the service. He had grown in his relationship with Christ, but having been in business for himself for three years, the pressures of business had caused him to miss most Sundays at church. Being single and having good looks proved to be detriments.

When I met with Ted, he had been out of fellowship with Christ and other believers for almost three years. For the past year he had been sexually involved with a woman who worked for his company. It all came crashing down when her estranged husband caught them red-handed and an altercation ensued. Ted went into deep depression over his guilt, but thanks to the care of his best friend, he expressed a desire to repent and turn around his life. But he didn't know how to change his life, so they came to my office to talk about the situation. The relationship between Ted and the woman was history, but he was left shipwrecked spiritually.

I'll never forget Ted's words to me. "I want to come back to God...if He will have a dirty, filthy sinner." His regret, contrition, and sincerity were genuine. He was broken over his sin, and after going through scripture after scripture speaking of the wideness of God's mercy and grace, we began several sessions which I told him were the "steps back to purity."

Often when Christian men allow their relationships with God to grow cold, the first place Satan attacks is the flesh. The backslidden man is usually tempted with sexual sin, the weakest link in his spiritual chain. It doesn't matter whether it comes in the form of fantasy, pornography, or actual participation, fleshly temptation will occur. If a man is to get his life back on track he needs to deal ruthlessly with this area of his life. Here there can be no fuzziness, no ambiguity, and no indecisiveness.

With the help of his best friend, I took Ted through a step-by-step process to regain his purity. If you're having trouble getting back on track in, or because of, this area, please follow these steps.

1. Confess sin as sin and call it sin.

As long as you minimize it, relabel it, or rationalize it, you can't be helped. You need to acknowledge sexual lust as sin, confess it to God, and claim your forgiveness according to 1 John 1:9. The more you minimize or deny it, the longer you defer dealing with it effectively. The Bible says, "For everything in the world—the cravings of sinful man, the lust of his eyes and the boasting of what he has and does—comes not from the Father but from the world" (1 John 2:16). Lusting in your mind and flesh is not of God, but of the world and its system. Therefore it is sin. As long as you call it something else you are in denial, and the longer it will take to get back on track.

"He who conceals his sins does not prosper, but whoever confesses and renounces them finds mercy" (Proverbs 28:13). In Psalm 32, David said that when he failed to confess or declare his sin, his body wasted away. Your physical health is affected by your spiritual health. Don't wait. Confess your sin to God and get back on track toward purity.

2. Confess sin to a trusted brother.

You may be thinking, "Wait a minute! Isn't confession to God enough?" It may be, but if you have a close friend who loves you, warts and all, you not only should confess the problem to God, but to your friend as well. Though Ted's buddy didn't want to hear all the steamy details, Ted trusted him enough to tell him of repeated trysts with this woman. It was not easy, but for Ted, it was very necessary.

"Therefore, confess your sins to each other, and pray for each other so that you may be healed" (James 5:16). This is what close Christian brothers are for, to hear you and love you, though you have violated God's standard. Not only is there a powerful release that comes from doing this, but that trusted brother then knows how to pray for you. Confession brings healing to your soul. It will also allow your friend to encourage you and build you up. Accountability can begin, which is something we all need. This is a difficult step for many, but if you are serious about getting your life on track, confess your sin to a Christian friend in whom you trust.

3. Get rid of all reminders.

When getting back on track, you need to abandon all reminders that lured you away from Christ. If you've read or watched things in the past that took you down the road of impurity, get rid of them. If you have developed friendships with others who are into impurity, part company with them immediately. Paul was right when he said "bad company corrupts good character" (1 Corinthians 15:33). We soon begin to think like, act like, and talk like those we are around. I've had people tell me, "Now that I'm getting stronger in the Lord, I can be around those people and have an influence on them." That may be so, but make sure you're strong enough in the Lord so the influence won't go the other way. I have seen strong Christians bring lost sinners to Christ, and I have seen weak Christians have their lives destroyed by evil.

In cases where Christians have fallen into impurity with someone they work with, drastic measures have to be taken to remove themselves from the daily temptation and reminders. Occasionally an individual will even quit a job to keep out of an unhealthy situation. Though Ted didn't like the idea, he eventually transferred to another site to keep from having to face the temptation that took him down the first time. Men have a notion that they are strong and invincible, and once they determine something, nothing will lure them away. Unfortunately, the fact is most of us aren't like that at all. Those who have sinned sexually have a strong propensity to be lured into the impure when the opportunity is present. It takes being steeped in God's Word and good accountability with another Christian to keep that from happening. Furthermore, you need to get rid of any correspondence, pictures, and trinkets you may have to remind you of the period of impurity in your life.

4. Avoid watching anything on television that is sensual.

The Bible warns us to "avoid every kind of evil" (1 Thessalonians 5:22). The Amplified Bible pointedly translates that in a vivid way: "Abstain from evil (shrink from it, and keep aloof from it) in whatever form or whatever kind it may be."

This simply means we are to be extremely selective about what we watch and when we watch it. Most constraints on programming have been lifted, and sensual scenes are shown at little or no discretion by the network or cable company. The discretion must be made by you.

5. Place a big emphasis on loving your spouse exclusively.

I have two offices, one at home and one at church. In prominent places on both desks are rather large pictures of my lovely wife. No matter where I place those pictures, her eyes are looking into mine. Believe me, that keeps even my thought life under control.

Proverbs 5 is probably the most blatant place in scripture that admonishes men to be true in thought and deed to our mates.

> Drink water from your own cistern, running water from your own well. Should your springs overflow in the streets, your streams of water in the public squares? Let them be yours alone, never to be shared with strangers. May your fountain be blessed, and may you rejoice in the wife of your youth (Proverbs 5:15-18).

The whole theme of that passage is to love your partner exclusively, in thought and deed. When you're trying to get back on track morally in your life, you need to...

> Call your wife several times throughout the day.
> Leave love notes to her where she'll find them.
> Send flowers when it's not a birthday or an anniversary.
> Be with her as much as you possibly can.
> Take her on a business trip now and then if you travel.
> Turn off the TV and talk with her.

I believe part of loving your wife as Christ loves the Church has to do with showing her undivided attention when you're

73

with her. If you allow the love of your wife to fill your mind, the lust for other women will dissipate.

6. Concentrate on those passages that deal with purity.

God's Word is a great antidote to impurity. In fact, David wrote, "How can a young man keep his way pure? By living according to your word" (Psalm 119:9). We need to hold tightly to that verse, because it says there is a definite connection between knowing God's Word and living a pure life before Him. A pattern of letting God's Word dwell in us richly from day to day (see Colossians 3:16) is insurance against impure thoughts and deeds taking hold in your life. You may never be free from temptation in this area, but you can be free from impurity dominating your thinking and conduct.

Other passages you may want to read daily include: 2 Peter 1:3-11; Colossians 3:1; 1 Thessalonians 4:1-8; 1 Corinthians 6:18; Ephesians 5:3-5; Psalm 1; Philippians 4:8.

Focus and meditate on these passages. It would even be helpful to memorize them. Getting back on track is God's will for your life, especially in the important area of purity. If you don't get a handle on this area of your life, it has a way of coloring every area.

Many years ago, when I was a new Christian, an elderly saint of God gave me the following prayer. I've treasured its wisdom many times.

Lord, cleanse my mind that all my thoughts be pure;
Lord, refine my speech, that all my words be clean;
Lord, refocus my eyes that my vision be holy;
Lord, re-aim my feet to destinations that are right;
Lord, re-tune my ears to listen to the sanctified;
Lord, let my whole life reflect your holiness!

It's a prayer worth praying and a theme worthy of reflection. You'll be glad to know that while Ted has a lot of growing to do, he's back on track and has built into his life some solid safe-guards to keep him from stumbling again. He's wise enough to know not to become over-confident, but he is living a pure lifestyle, day by day. May your trip back be just as strong!

Getting Back on Track

What are the purity issues you need to clean up in your life?

Can you confess them to God as sin?

Can you confess them to a trusted Christian friend?

What reminders do you need to get rid of?

What things do you need to avoid in the future?

How will building your marriage help you in personal purity?

Chapter Eight

Getting Back on Track Through Settled Differences

PEOPLE WHO ARE SERIOUS ABOUT getting back on track have a price to pay. Some believe the biggest part of that price is clearing the ledger of differences we have with others.

Jack was a man in his late forties who had been fairly successful in a retail business. He was a quiet man, who seldom spoke and always had a furrowed brow as if something were bothering him. He was mostly inactive at church, but would come on special occasions to please his wife. One day she told me that when they had lived in another city, Jack had been a pillar in their church. He had been the chairman of that church's governing board, belonged to a professional business-man's organization, and given his testimony many times. She asked if I would take him to lunch and see if I could say something that would challenge him to "get back on track." I agreed.

We met at a private club and had a table to ourselves away from everyone else. That was a good thing, for what I thought would be a one-hour lunch turned into a three-hour session. Jack told me his story. While they had been active in that church, he had gone into business with another "pillar" of the church who turned out to be extremely dishonest. Jack lost not only his share of the company, but was stuck with over $35,000 in improvements that his partner had failed to pay. It devastated him. They lost their home, their cars, and came within an inch of filing for bankruptcy. At nearly forty years old he had to start over again in a menial job until he could save enough money to begin anew in the business. Jack became very bitter toward that business partner, quit the church, and subsequently moved to our city. While his business was a success again, and he had paid back every dime of the debt, he was a miserable man, still harboring bitterness against the former business partner.

I was the first man he had spilled everything to in ten years. While I could see some of the tenseness leave his face, I still saw a defeated man, shot down by his own refusal to let go of a ten-year-old grudge. In tears, however, he said to me, "Pastor, I want to recover what I once had when I was serving the Lord, but there doesn't seem to be any way to get it back." I think he knew he would never "get it back" until he dissolved the differences he had and forgave the man who had hurt him. While he assented to that mentally, he was in a form of denial, refusing to deal with the issue emotionally.

Getting back on track spiritually requires settling differences, forgiving the offender, and getting on with God. That's hard to do. Jack needed to clean the slate, reestablish his relationships, and get the weight of bitterness off his back. Somehow, he needed to settle his differences with his former partner.

I believe there are at least five steps one must take if he wants to get back on track in this area. As in a recipe, you can't leave one ingredient out and expect the cake to be any good. You can't leave even one of these steps out and expect to get back on track. But if you follow through with this process, you will find a recipe for settling differences that really works.

1. Recognize there are no shortcuts.

You may paint over a stain and get away with it on wood, but you cannot cover a broken or bruised relationship. You can't rationalize it away by saying, "It's been so long, it doesn't matter." You can't justify your refusal by saying, "It was his fault, so it's his place to come to me." You may believe it's not a factor, that you don't think about it anymore and it's a non-issue. Unfortunately, that's exactly what Satan wants you to think while he plants that offense ever deeper into your spirit. Like a splinter in a finger, it hurts to cut it out, but to leave it in will bring only more serious hurt and pain. Nor can you surmise, "He lives halfway across the country, so it's impossible to open up the issue again." Wrong! We do business with people for profit who are halfway across the country, we vacation at places halfway across the country, we order merchandise from people halfway across the country, so why shouldn't we make a wrong right, even if it's halfway across the country?

No matter how much you pretend or rationalize, the breech in the relationship is still there, and God won't bless until you've done everything you can do to mend the fence.

2. Quit living in the past.

People who nurse bitterness are really living in the past. They are taking one offensive event and "freezing" it in time.

You've moved on from other things in your past, like honest mistakes, poor judgments, and bad investments, so why not move on from this, too? We somehow think we are punishing the offender by allowing this wedge to continue. There is an old Indian proverb that says, "No man steps into the same river twice." Do you know why that is true? Because the river is flowing. The water you stepped into yesterday is a hundred miles downstream today, so when you step into that river today, you are really stepping into another river. Time moves on and so do we. Paul said it succinctly: "But one thing I do: Forgetting what is behind" (Philippians 3:13).

We don't buy a cup of coffee for a nickel anymore, or get a haircut for $1.50, or buy a newspaper for a dime. Everything changes. He who lives in the past is miserable in the present and has no future. If you want to get back on track, quit living in the past.

3. A held grudge damages your relationship with God.

Our horizontal relationships with others affect our vertical relationship with God. That's why Jesus said,

> Therefore, if you are offering your gift at the altar and there remember that your brother has something against you, leave your gift there in front of the altar. First go and be reconciled to your brother; then come and offer your gift (Matthew 5:23-24).

Jesus is saying you can't even worship God properly as long as there is a rift between you and your brother. He forbids you to worship God, telling you to leave, take care of unfinished business, then come and offer your gift. It doesn't matter who caused the offense. In fact, notice that Jesus even said if your brother has something against you, go and take care of it. His point is clear: You cannot be in a right relationship with God as long as you're in an adversarial relationship with your brother.

That's why Peter told us to live considerately with our wives, treating them with respect so that our prayers may not be hindered (1 Peter 3:7). If you're in an adversarial relationship with your spouse, your relationship to God is deeply affected. This is why you cannot get back on track with God and still harbor a grudge.

4. We are forbidden by Scripture to retaliate.

Peter goes on to say, "Do not repay evil with evil or insult with insult" (1 Peter 3:9). Jesus made it clear in the sermon on the mount that if you are slapped on the right cheek, you are to turn the other cheek to your offender (see Matthew 5:39). We're also told in that same chapter that we are to love our enemies, not just our friends. If we love only those who love us, what more are we doing than non-believers?

In teaching us to follow Christ's example, Peter says, "When they hurled their insults at him, he did not retaliate; when he suffered, he made no threats. Instead he entrusted himself to him who judges justly" (1 Peter 2:23). If Jesus did that, and He is our example, then we are to do the same. Retaliation doesn't work. The Bible says, "'It is mine to avenge; I will repay,' says the Lord" (Romans 12:19). If we attempt repayment, we'll only botch it up. God has not called you to be the chairman of the vengeance committee. That's His department. He'll do it well, because He alone knows all the facts. Solomon was right when he said, "Do not say, 'I'll pay you back for this wrong!' Wait for the LORD, and he will deliver you" (Proverbs 20:22).

Many think they are properly retaliating by holding everything inside and keeping the grudge alive. Of course, when you do that, you only hurt yourself. It creates a bitterness in your soul, drives the poison of resentment into your spirit, and keeps you from close fellowship with the Lord.

5. Make a conscious commitment to forgive.

"Oh, that's easy to say, but hard to do." Friend, I didn't say it would be easy. However, there is some motivation. If you're having trouble forgiving your offender, just remember all of the things for which God has forgiven you. That's why Paul wrote the words, "Be kind and compassionate to one another, forgiving each other, just as in Christ God forgave you" (Ephesians 4:32). God forgave you of every offense, every bad thought, every evil motive and deed.

You may be saying, as did Jack, "But the rift occurred because he was clearly in the wrong. He was the offender and I was the offended. It's his place to come and ask me for forgiveness." Sorry, but that's not how it works. You have a responsibility to go to him and ask his forgiveness for harboring hatred toward him. What he does with that is up to him. What God does with that will be amazing.

When the poet Edwin Markham came to his retirement years, he discovered his banker had defrauded him of all his retirement funds. In his bitterness, Markham could no longer write poetry. He became morose, sour, and unfruitful. He would sit for hours but nothing would come. His bitterness had emptied his life of joy and happiness. Then one day while doodling at his desk, he began to draw some circles. Suddenly, he was deeply convicted by the Holy Spirit and wrote:

> He drew a circle that shut me out,
> Heretic, rebel, a thing to flout;
> But love and I had the wit to win,
> We drew a circle that took him in.

Edwin Markham knew what he was talking about. Love is a very powerful thing. God doesn't want the sun to set on our wrath. If you are at odds with anyone, whether he is a fellow Christian or not, go now and right the wrong. Humble yourself before him, let him know you don't want to go on living like you're living. It will glorify God!

Maybe it's time for you to draw a bigger circle than your offender has drawn. I remember an elderly preacher once told me, "Love and forgive your enemies...it will drive them nuts."

What is forgiveness? Let's begin with what it is not. Forgiveness is not pretending the offense never happened. Nor is it excusing unacceptable behavior, nor is it endorsing sin. It is not putting the incident out of your mind, or sweeping it under the rug. *Forgiveness is releasing the offender from your demand of paying you for the offense.*

You may grimace under that definition, but the key phrase is *your demand*. It doesn't mean the offender is released from an obligation to make right the wrong he did, but that you will no longer hold him responsible for it. Now it's the Lord's responsibility. I'll admit that isn't easy to do, especially when a lot of time has passed. But your forgiveness unlocks a prison cell that has held you for all this time. How he or she responds to your forgiveness places the ball in the offender's court. It's no longer your concern. What is important is that you have done the right and biblical thing.

Now you may be saying, "What if he does the same thing again? Am I supposed to forgive him again?" As a matter of fact, yes you are! Peter asked Jesus an important question in Matthew 18 that settles this issue once and for all.

> Then Peter came to Jesus and asked, "Lord, how many times shall I forgive my brother when he sins against me? Up to seven times?" Jesus answered, "I tell you, not seven times, but seventy-seven times" (Matthew 18:21-22).

Believe me, that is not what Peter wanted to hear! What Jesus is really teaching here is that He expects us, who have been fully and freely forgiven by Him, to practice unlimited forgiveness in our lives. Remember Jack? Well, it took some time, but without telling anyone, he caught a plane to the city where his old business partner lived, walked into his office, and asked his forgiveness for harboring such a grudge. The previous partner melted, even wept, and the two men embraced. The last word I heard was that Jack was being paid back a little at a time by that man—not at Jack's insistence, but by the miraculous power of humbling oneself to another.

Maybe there is a breach between you and someone in your past that has never been resolved. The best time to resolve it is now. The best reason to do it is that it will allow you to get back on track and get on with your Christian walk.

O God, I confess to you that I have held this grudge long enough. Cleanse me from bitterness and hatred. Give me the courage to do now what I should have done long ago, to go to _____ and ask for forgiveness. Amen.

Getting Back on Track

With whom do you need to settle differences?

Are you willing to give up your grudge and your desire to retaliate?

How does harboring a grudge damage your spiritual life?

If you could settle the difference, how would you do it?

What two practical steps could you do to settle the issue?

Chapter Nine

Getting Back on Track Through Ministry to Others

DARYL WAS ONE OF THE MOST effective men I've ever known. His profession didn't seem to fit his looks and personality. He was a foreman in a large food warehouse from 6:30 A.M. to 3:30 P.M. during the week, but three evenings a week he turned into another man. He was a motivator of men and seemed to be gifted as a pied piper. Men were attracted to him and had no problem following him. To say he was an effective leader is almost an understatement. Daryl led a men's Bible study, headed up a crew of guys who repaired single mothers' cars one Saturday each month, and was a superb evangelist, constantly witnessing to other guys and leading them to Christ.

Then suddenly he disappeared. I no longer saw him at any of the church functions. When I asked about him, I sadly discovered that Daryl had gone over the line with a lady he was dating. In a moment of weakness he did what he warned guys in his discipleship group to never do: commit immorality. It was a one-time mistake, but Daryl was devastated. He quit everything he was doing, broke off all contact with the woman, and dropped out of sight. For two years he lived in total remorse.

He finally developed the courage to contact one of the men with whom he had a great influence, to find out how he could get back on track. He had literally repented for two years, felt he was forgiven, and wanted more than anything to make his life count for Christ again. In his words, "Coming back to church was fine, but God didn't save me to sit. He saved me to serve." Daryl slowly immersed himself in serving the Lord by serving others again, and though he's moved out of the area, he is still serving the Lord to this day.

Daryl learned something that few learn. God didn't save us just so we could say we have salvation. If that were the case, He would have taken us to heaven immediately after we were saved. Try as we may, we're not back on track unless we are in ministry to others in the body of Christ. Otherwise, we become nothing more than spectators. Any significant coming back into close fellowship with Christ will involve a commitment to serve. Do you need to know how to get back on track in this area?

1. Understand body life.

It all begins by grasping the concept of body life. In 1 Corinthians 12, Paul likens the Church to a human body. He reminds us that just as a human body has many parts, each with a unique function, so the Church as the body of Christ has many parts, and each person is a member of that body. In a human body, the arm has a different function than the leg, which has a different function than the tongue, which has a different function than the foot, the ear, and the pancreas. There are many parts, each with differing functions, yet all belonging to one body. When they work together in proper balance, they form a strong, healthy body.

When you were saved, God placed you in the body of Christ to "occupy" until He returns. He assigned you a post of duty—a ministry—and He fully expects you to stay faithful to that post. When a person wanders away from God, the first thing to go is his service. That's why it must be among the first things to do when you come back. In grasping the concept of body life, God would have us understand some truths. First, not everyone has the same task or function in the body of Christ. Each individual's role is unique and important. No one should feel inferior in the body because of his function. In 1 Corinthians 12, Paul draws some comparisons. He says if a foot should say, "Because I am not a hand, I do not belong to the body," that would not make it cease to be a part of the body. Of course, you can understand why a foot might feel inferior. It carries all the weight of the body, is usually enclosed in a sock, and has no particular beauty about it. But Paul's point is that the foot has a very important function, even though it's not similar to the hand.

So it is with us. I can't get up and sing a beautiful solo, but I can teach a class. Maybe you can't teach a class, but you can drive a bus for the youth, or help the church with its remodeling job, or type the bulletin. God does the arranging of the various parts and functions: "But in fact, God has arranged the parts in the body, every one of them, just as he wanted them to be" (1 Corinthians 12:18). That's why God doesn't give any one person all the gifts. Like a master conductor of the symphony orchestra, He needs the brass, the percussion, the strings, and the reeds to create a complete sound. They are all equally important. Can you imagine an orchestra with only drums? It wouldn't work!

We members of the body are interdependent with each other. We are not independent of each other, but interdependent, relying on one another. That's why Paul said, "The eye cannot say to the hand, 'I don't need you!' And the head cannot say to the feet, 'I don't need you'" (1 Corinthians 12:21). We need each other as we serve in the body of Christ.

2. Every believer is gifted in the body of Christ.

Paul says in 1 Corinthians 12:7 that "to each one the manifestation of the Spirit is given for the common good." In other words, no one has been left out. In Romans 12:6 he further says, "We have different gifts, according to the grace given us." Note that he said "we have," not "if we have." We have the gifts. That's why 1 Peter 4:10 says, "Each one should use whatever gift he has received to serve others."

The Bible teaches that God left no one out when He handed out spiritual gifts. Everyone has at least one spiritual gift, and I contend that most believers have two or three. Sometimes it takes us a long time to discover what our area of giftedness is, but we have all been gifted. Between 1 Corinthians 12, Romans 12, and Ephesians 4, we have a listing of what some of those gifts are. They range from the sign gifts: tongues, interpretation of tongues, miracles, and healings; all the way to service gifts: giving, faith, encouragement, and helps. Though we won't go into a technical meaning of all the gifts, here are a few that may help you find your niche.

- Administration - for those who like to plan and organize things.
- Leadership - for those who like to motivate others and challenge people.
- Service - for those who like to do things behind the scenes for others.

- Teaching - for those who like to impart God's Word to others.
- Evangelism - for those who enjoy talking to others about receiving Christ.
- Apostles - for those who aspire to be missionaries in cross-cultural settings.
- Giving - for those who like detecting need and filling it in others.
- Mercy - for those who enjoy counseling others or visiting the sick and elderly.
- Exhortation - for those who like encouraging others and get fulfillment from it.
- Discerning - for those who like apologetics and exposing heretical teachings.

There are others, but those are enough to get you excited about serving in the body of Christ. Serving keeps you from becoming just a consumer in the Church. Many people today only consume and never give out. It's no wonder someone has said, "If your intake exceeds your output, your upkeep will be your downfall."

If all you do is partake of the teachings, enjoy the music, revel in the fellowship, but don't serve, you will become spiritually obese porkers with no use to anyone in the kingdom. I'm not saying you shouldn't consume, but along with it you need avenues of service to work out what God has worked into you.

Because of the teachings of Jesus, we shouldn't wonder that God wants us to serve in the Body of Christ. "Just as the Son of Man did not come to be served, but to serve, and to give his life as a ransom for many" (Matthew 20:28). If we are the extension of Christ, the true role of the Church on earth, our attitude needs to be the same as His. Jesus was sold on service.

Perhaps you are wondering what God would have you do in your church. Below is a list, not meant to be exhaustive by any means, with several ideas for serving in your local church. Take a pen and put a check by the two or three things you think might interest you.

___ Ushering
___ Greeting at the door
___ Singing in the choir
___ Operating the sound equipment
___ Driving the church bus or van
___ Helping with parking in the parking lot
___ Working with the church finances
___ Writing articles for the church newspaper
___ Helping counsel troubled people
___ Teaching a Sunday school class
___ Hosting a Bible study group in your home
___ Volunteering to do yard work for the church premises
___ Visiting unsaved people to share the gospel with them
___ Visiting in nursing and retirement homes
___ Working in the nursery
___ Teaching in pre-school classes
___ Working with children or teens
___ Helping with inner-city mission work
___ Challenging others at prayer breakfasts
___ Working with young couples to develop good marriages

There are many areas of need in your local church. I suggest you go to one of your pastors and ask him where the biggest need for workers is right now.

For a number of years, I've kept a prayer in the front of my Bible. I have no idea who authored it, but I think it expresses the importance of service extremely well. I hope you'll do more than just read the prayer—I hope you'll make it your very own.

Lord, I'm willing to receive what you give,
To relinquish what you take,
To suffer what you allow,

To be what you require,
To do what you command.

Getting Back on Track

What do you think are your spiritual gifts?

Where do you most enjoy serving?

What are you burdened by in your world?

What do you think is God's call in your life?

Where are you needed?

What do you feel qualified to do?

Chapter Ten

Getting Back on Track Through Witnessing

THE VERY SOUND OF THE WORD scares the wits out of most Christians—witnessing! When I helped facilitate Brad's journey back to the Lord, after being in spiritual limbo for almost six years, witnessing was the hardest step for him to reincorporate.

Brad's story is not uncommon for Christian men. After being married for almost ten years, Brad messed up big time. He and his wife, childhood sweethearts, simply drifted apart by neglect and busyness. Brad met a woman at work who gladly listened to his tale of woe about not being appreciated by his wife, how he was starved for affection, and that he felt he needed to find himself. All of this occurred despite the fact he came to know the Lord at age twenty-two, about two years before he was married. He not only attended church, but took part in the men's ministry and even took an evangelism course. Brad was fairly effective in influencing his friends for Christ, and was responsible for leading three or four of his buddies to faith in Jesus. But when his marital woes befell him, he dropped out of everything. When his relationship with his "friend" at work evolved into a full-blown affair, he realized he was going to lose his wife and two children. So Brad did a drastic about-face, repented, and through a couples' discipleship class got back into fellowship with the Lord.

As we talked over lunch, I asked Brad if he was ready to get back into witnessing regularly and rejoining our calling program. Brad froze. "Anything else!" he moaned. "I'll do anything but that. I feel totally unworthy to talk to others about Christ when I've made such a mess of my own life." But in the same breath, he fully acknowledged that he needed to start sharing his faith again. So I struck a deal with him; I offered to take him with me on my next three gospel presentation calls. It worked! The very first call we made, a man about Brad's age whose wife had left him, came to Christ while kneeling in his living room. That brought back Brad's old fire. He reentered the witnessing program and returned to being very effective in influencing others until a job change took him out of state. The last I heard, his marriage is growing and his witnessing is on fire.

A definite part of getting back on track is developing a desire and determination to be salt and light to other people. Because every individual has a different personality and temperament—some are introverts and some extroverts, some charismatic and some aren't—sharing Christ will be done differently by different people. Be that as it may, there are some principles we need to understand about witnessing.

1. Be absolutely sure of your own salvation.

This is where witnessing starts. You have to *know* you're saved and safe in salvation before you can tell anyone else about it. "I write these things to you who believe in the name of the Son of God so that you may know that you have eternal life" (1 John 5:13). That verse has been like the North Star for me in my own walk with Christ. It nails down the assurance that God wants me to have. Another verse I memorized years ago also offers me assurance: "I tell you the truth, he who believes has everlasting life" (John 6:47). Notice the present tense of the verb "has." It means I have salvation *now*.

This assurance is absolutely necessary if you are going to have a lasting influence on anyone else. Otherwise, you'll be like the vacuum cleaner salesman who told a prospect, "This is a good cleaner, though I personally use another brand." That won't work. Unless you are totally sure, absolutely convinced that Christ has saved you, you won't be very convincing.

2. Have a clear and personal testimony.

The word "testimony" scares people. They conjure up some detailed, polished speech about Christ and our relationship to Him. But an effective testimony is a personal, concise statement about what actually happened to you.

A good testimony has three major parts:

> *Before* you came to Christ,
> *How* you came to Christ, and
> *Since* you came to Christ.

I think about 10 percent should be devoted to your life before meeting Christ. You might mention your condition, your need, your insecurity. There is no need for detailed descriptions of the horrible sins you committed. Just give a clear statement of your condition prior to knowing Christ.

Another 10 percent needs to tell the story of how you came to Christ. Again, exact details aren't as important as the moment of crisis through which you passed as you came to believe and accept Him.

That leaves 80 percent of your testimony to tell the story of what has happened in your life since you came to know Christ. Give specific examples of what has changed. It was the changed lives of the apostles that influenced the people around them. Tell your friends how your life has changed; there are very few things in our world which can so profoundly alter a life.

I recently heard a testimony that followed this general formula. It was shared at a businessman's breakfast, and it went something like this: "I was raised in a non-Christian home and basically never went to church. As I got older, got married, and had a family, I developed an empty feeling, as though I had a vacuum in my life. I made a lot of money, drove a nice car, lived in a nice home, and outwardly had it all together, but I was slowly dying on the inside from a lack of fulfillment.

"Then I met a manufacturer's representative from Atlanta, and we seemed to hit it off fairly well. After a sales meeting, we went for coffee and he asked me if I was sure I was going to heaven when I died. I couldn't give him an answer, and it made me think. When my boss invited me to visit his church, I knew I was being drawn into something deeply significant. Finally my boss asked if I would be willing to invite Christ into my life. I did, right in my office. There were no bells, whistles, or streaks of lightning, but since I made that decision, I've had a peace and tranquillity in my life I've never had before. I also found a purpose for my life that makes me excited about getting up every day. My marriage is better, my health is better, and my outlook is better. I'm learning much from the Bible about how to live victoriously and fight temptation successfully, which I was never able to do before. I wonder now how I ever made it through without Christ."

That testimony, by a forty-year-old businessman, deeply affected a half dozen men at that breakfast who, that very morning, gave their hearts to the Lord! Your personal testimony should be just that simple. You don't have to be a theological wizard, a Bible scholar, or a trained apologist. You just have to articulate as best you can what the Lord has done in your life. Someone has said, "Evangelism is one poor beggar telling another poor beggar where to find bread." Your testimony doesn't have to be glamorous, colorful, or creative—just authentic. It has been well said, "You either have a testimony or you need to hear one."

3. Witness in the power of the Holy Spirit.

God never gives us a task to do without first providing the power to do it. The same is true in the task of telling others the good news. You don't do it in your own power or by your own ability to charm, convince, or "wow" others. You tell the truth, and you allow the Holy Spirit to work through you.

Shortly after I became a Christian, a well meaning person said to me, "Bob, you're not really a Christian unless you tell others how they can find Christ." I was horrified of the thought of bringing that topic up to my friends, much less complete strangers. Then I learned a couple of truths. First, I learned that God simply wanted me to tell others about what I found in Jesus Christ and that they could find it too. Second, I learned I didn't have to tell them in my own power. Listen to the words the risen Christ gave His apostles: "But you will receive power when the Holy Spirit comes on you; and you will be my witnesses" (Acts 1:8).

What a great promise! If someone ordered me to put a jumbo jet 37,000 feet up in the air, I'd have two choices. I could get behind the plane and push, hoping to get enough speed to become airborne, or I could start the engines and allow their thrust to lift the plane off the ground. As a pilot, I'd have to rely on the power of those engines. It's the same for us; sometimes we have to rely on someone else's power. In witnessing, you have two options: to do it in your own strength (and fail), or to do it trusting the power of the Holy Spirit. That's the way God says it has to be done. It won't take you long to figure out which one is easier and more effective. Most of us are conditioned by our culture to do everything ourselves. It's the American way to say, "I did it my way." But in witnessing, we must do it God's way, and that means relying on His strength rather than our own.

The chief fear of witnessing is that we won't know what to say. We fear getting started in a conversation, then suddenly being asked a question we can't answer. We're afraid we'll just stand there with our mouths open, looking stupid and convincing the person we're talking to that all Christians are bumbling fools. But you know, there is a great promise God gave to Jeremiah which you can apply to your own life when you're obeying the command to be a witness:

> But the LORD said to me, "Do not say, 'I am only a child.' You must go to everyone I send you to and say whatever I command you. Do not be afraid of them, for I am with you and will rescue you," declares the LORD. Then the LORD reached out his hand and touched my mouth and said to me, "Now I have put my words in your mouth" (Jeremiah 1:7-9).

Now, that is a promise! God will put the right words in your mouth when you need them! Of course, that doesn't relieve you from the responsibility to know your Bible and understand the gospel. The clearer the gospel is in your own mind, the easier it will be for you to share it. That leads to the next principle.

4. Understand the message of the gospel.

The word "gospel" is from a Greek word meaning "good news." In the original language it referred to the message of the evangelist or the courier who would ride through the village and shout public announcements. The good news of the gospel can be summed up in one sentence: God has brought about our salvation by allowing His Son, Jesus, to die on the cross, rise again, and pay the penalty for our sins, so by our faith in His finished work, we receive the gift of eternal life, forgiveness of sins, and abundant life here and now. That's the good news.

There is a progression in the gospel story that goes like this: need, provision, acceptance.

The need. People need salvation because we all are sinners by nature (Ephesians 2:1). We have broken God's perfect law, and thus we are under a curse (Galatians 3:10). Not only are we sinners, there is nothing we can do to change that condition. Man is completely helpless and hopeless to alter, improve, or change his sinful condition. "'Although you wash yourself with soda and use an abundance of soap, the stain of your guilt is still before me,' declares the Sovereign LORD" (Jeremiah 2:22). Mankind tries to save himself, but we can never change enough to perfectly obey God's law. Again, the book of Jeremiah says, "Can the Ethiopian change his skin or the leopard its spots? Neither can you do good who are accustomed to doing evil" (Jeremiah 13:23). So man is sinful and separated from God.

The provision. While we can't save ourselves, God has intervened and offered a provision to meet our needs. We are told that in the fullness of time, God sent forth His Son, born under the law, to redeem those under the law (see Galatians 4:4). While we can't change our "spots" or the indelible stain of sin, God can. We can't pay the penalty demanded by sin, but Jesus did by dying on the cross.

The acceptance. This is the simplest part, but the place where most people get hung up. It's by faith, placed in the finished work of Christ on the cross and the empty tomb, that we accept God's provision for our need. Saving faith is not mere intellectual assent, or propositional truth. It is not merely the acceptance of the fact that Jesus died, rose again, and ascended back to God. We're told in James 2:19 that even the demons believe the story of God. They believe it, but they aren't committed to it. If all we do is merely assent to that truth, we are no better off than the demons.

Saving faith involves two things, trusting Christ alone and committing your life to Him. Putting all your confidence for salvation in Christ alone means you are not trusting in anything else, just Jesus Christ and what He did for you on the cross. Saving faith means you are willing to commit yourself wholly to Jesus Christ. If you're on the fourth floor of a burning building, sitting on the window ledge with flames lapping at your back, and the firefighters below yell at you to jump into the net, you can say, "I believe you'll catch me," but if you don't commit yourself to that belief by actually jumping, you'll lose your life. Salvation means you trust Christ and you commit to Him.

Whether it's your testimony or a systematic presentation of the gospel, you will eventually need to say to people to whom you're witnessing, "Would you like to receive Jesus Christ right now?" You see, people have to make a decision. God requires us to repent of sin (see Luke 13:3) and confess the name of Christ (see Romans 10:9-10). If you are going to witness, you might as well make up your mind right now that you'll soon be asking someone this question. It's the purpose of witnessing. When it comes to personally assuming the responsibility to be a faithful witness, you need only to be reminded that God's ordained way of getting the good news out is through human tongues telling, attached to human beings changed.

I once read of a man who won five million dollars in his state's lottery. Normally a quiet and introverted individual, he ran up and down the streets of his city for almost an hour yelling at the top of his voice, "Look what happened to me!" He had some good news all right, and he indiscriminately was willing to abandon decorum and let it out. While overnight wealth obviously changed this man's lifestyle, it was only for a while. It was only money, and it was confined to this life. Something greater and more profound has changed my life, and I too must tell it. Getting back on track must include witnessing to others.

Maybe by now you're wondering how to get started. I've listed below some practical things you can do to get back on track in this area.

First, begin a prayer list of unsaved people. I have such a list, and I pray for those people every Wednesday and at other times as often as I can think to. I want the people in my life to know the cleansing power of the blood of Jesus, and a written list keeps them on my mind.

Second, ask God daily to help you seize opportunities. I've found that if I ask God to cross my path with someone who needs the Lord, He will do it. My problem is identifying who and where those people are in my daily activities. Maybe you're wondering who those people are in your world. They might include your banker, the check-out clerk at the supermarket, your mail carrier, your bus driver, your mechanic, your doctor, the repair man who comes to your house, the person next to you on your next flight, your next-door neighbor, your boss, your secretary, your waiter, your barber—the list is endless. Remember, God is faithful and wants you to be a light to those whose path you cross.

Third, carry some clear, understandable tracts you can leave with people. Ask your pastor or Sunday school teacher for these. I'm never caught without a short, clear tract on how people can find salvation. God will honor your attempts. Remember, His Word does not return empty, but accomplishes what God wants (see Isaiah 55:11).

Getting Back on Track

Are you sure of your salvation?

Have you ever written out your personal testimony? (If not, follow the outline above and write it out now.)

Who are you praying will come to Christ?

To whom do you want to tell your testimony?

If someone asked you to explain the gospel, what would you say?

Chapter Eleven

Getting Back on Track Through Major Housecleaning

"TODAY IS GARBAGE DAY," Ted told me as we talked on the phone. Ted was in the process of getting his life back on track with God. His statement puzzled me, so I asked him what in the world was "garbage day?" He explained that every Friday was his personal garbage day—the day he dumped out of his life the junk that shouldn't be there. He would name the sin to be dumped and say, "Out you go, you don't belong here."

That may sound like an absurd way to eliminate sin, but however we do it, it needs to be done. I think Paul had this sort of housecleaning in mind when he wrote:

Put to death, therefore, whatever belongs to your earthly nature: sexual immorality, impurity, lust, evil desires and greed, which is idolatry. But now you must rid yourselves of all such things as these: anger, rage, malice, slander, and filthy language from your lips. Do not lie to each other, since you have taken off your old self with its practices, and have put on the new self, which is being renewed in knowledge in the image of its Creator. Here there is no Greek or Jew, circumcised or uncircumcised, barbarian, Scythian, slave or free, but Christ is all, and is in all (Colossians 3:5,8-11).

When you read that passage carefully, you discover Paul is calling for us to get rid of quite a number of things. He mentions sexual immorality, impurity, lust, evil desires, anger, malice, bad language, lying, and prejudice—all things we should dump out of our lives on garbage day. Yet that's only the tip of the iceberg. In Ephesians 4, Paul has a similar list and talks about "putting off" sinful things. So whether you are putting it off, putting to death, or putting it in the garbage, you have to deal ruthlessly with those things in your life that keep you from full effectiveness with Christ.

I have always been intrigued with the story of the rich young ruler in Mark 10. Here is a young man who comes running to Jesus, which tells us how urgent and desperate he was. That's rather odd, because when you combine the accounts, we're told he was young, very wealthy, and had a key position in society. He had clout and probably great leadership abilities. But it was what he didn't have that concerned him. He was coming to Jesus looking for significance. His life, while filled with the knickknacks of pleasure seeking, was void of meaning and fulfillment. The Bible tells us he ran to Jesus, knelt down at His feet, and called the Lord a good teacher. Knowing that the young man was trying to attain fulfillment and righteousness by keeping the law, Jesus responded to his question, "What must I do to inherit eternal life?"

"Keep the commandments," Christ replied, knowing the young man had already tried that. He did this to show the man the utter futility of trying to find meaning in life by merely going through some religious motions. The young man responded, "I've kept all these from youth." His response became his own indictment. It was as if he were responding, "I did that, and it didn't work." Of course, Jesus knew the young man had not kept the law perfectly, or he wouldn't have been looking to Jesus for life. But the intriguing part of the story comes when Jesus says, "One thing you lack, go sell everything you have and give to the poor, and you will have treasure in heaven. Then come and follow me." That stopped the young ruler cold.

One thing you lack. In other words, there was one thing in his life standing between him and God. There was one obstacle between his desires and eternal significance. It was his money. What is it in your case? What one, two, or three things are still in your life, keeping you from fulfillment and effectiveness? They must go, whatever they are. They must be dumped out like so much garbage. Jesus will brook no rivals. He must come first in our lives, and anything within us that can't bow to Him must go. The fact is, even after we've accepted Christ as our Savior, debris creeps into our lives. There needs to be an occasional dumping of garbage, a regular housecleaning in your life.

About once a year in my own house, I gather up all the stuff that can't be used—stuff that is in the way or that has merely accumulated and is taking up space needed for the essentials—and I haul it to the dump. There need to be periods in our lives when we do the same thing; a spiritual housecleaning, if you please. Junk has a way of creeping in slowly, subtly, and unannounced. It needs to be dumped.

When Hezekiah decided to purify the temple, it had been in disrepair for years. People had brought things into it that were unholy. In 2 Chronicles 29 there is a description of the temple's condition:

> Remove all the defilement from the sanctuary. Our fathers were unfaithful; they did evil in the eyes of the LORD our God and forsook him. They turned their faces away from the LORD's dwelling place and turned their backs on him. They also shut the doors of the portico and put out the lamps. They did not burn incense or present any burnt offerings at the sanctuary to the God of Israel (2 Chronicles 29:5b-7).

The temple was in shambles. Something drastic had to be done to clean it up. The account goes on to read:

> The priests went into the sanctuary of the LORD to purify it. They brought out to the courtyard of the LORD's temple everything unclean that they found in the temple of the LORD. The Levites took it and carried it out to the Kidron Valley (2 Chronicles 29:16).

That's what I call a thorough housecleaning. The Bible tells us they began on the first day of the first month and didn't finish until the sixteenth day. Sixteen days of sweeping, pitching, washing, purifying, and clearing out the junk. Then, and only then, were they ready to celebrate the Passover.

There is a lesson here for you and me. If we are going to get back on track and stay on track, and if we're going to be effective for Christ, there needs to be a thorough housecleaning from time to time. Just as the rich young ruler had to get rid of his attachment to money before he could have a meaningful and effective relationship with Christ, so we must make a search and see what is in our lives that needs to go.

Maybe this is why I love to go back and read Psalm 139. I call it the "full-scale investigation" psalm. Here's how it begins:

O LORD, you have searched me and you know me. You know when I sit and when I rise; you perceive my thoughts from afar. You discern my going out and my lying down; you are familiar with all my ways (vv. 1-3).

That psalm goes on to say the all-seeing eye of God watches every part of our lives; nothing is hidden from Him. Furthermore, we cannot get away from His presence. Thus, we need to search our hearts with as much intensity as God does.

What needs to be pitched out of your life? Sexual lust? Love for money? Uncontrollable anger? Swearing and cursing? Alcohol? Drugs? Tobacco? Overeating? Gambling? Lying? Workaholism? A held grudge? The list may be long, but whatever it is, here are some practical steps to empower you to do a thorough job of house cleaning.

1. Acknowledge a cluttered life.

That's where housecleaning starts. Half the battle is won when you're willing to openly confess to God that you have things in your life that need to go. Denial is the enemy of wholeness. You can rationalize, justify, and evade the problem, but if you're honest and desperate enough, you'll admit you have junk in your life that needs to go.

After a stirring message in our church by a visiting evangelist, a man I'll call Tom came to the altar, knelt, and began to weep. God had convicted him of the fact that for two years he had been hooked on pornography. Magazines, videos, and tapes were stashed away in an office file where he worked, knowing if he ever brought it home he would be found out. He didn't trust himself to pitch it away as he re-dedicated himself to the Lord, so he asked one of the men praying over him to physically go with him and make sure it was all destroyed. That happened, and to this day, that man has kept that addictive poison out of his life. Does he still struggle at times? Yes, he's a healthy and handsome twenty-nine-year-old man whose glands are working overtime. But, it wasn't until he openly admitted the problem that he turned the corner and began to experience victory. What is cluttering your life? It begins with acknowledgment to yourself, your God, and perhaps a trusted confidant that there is garbage which must be cleaned out.

2. Determine it is your responsibility to sweep it out.

"Put to death," Paul says in Colossians. The command is issued to you. It does not say, "Ask God to do it for you." It's your job, your responsibility. You are to take the initiative. Of course, you can rationalize why the sin is there or blame it on a dysfunctional family, but the fact is, God wants you to take the initiative and assume responsibility for your own behavior. The popular thing today is to shift the blame for our actions onto someone else. But Scripture is consistent in saying we are to assume responsibility. In 1 Timothy 5:22 it says, "Keep yourselves pure." In 2 Timothy 4:5 we read, "Keep your head in all situations." Hebrews 13:5 says to "keep your lives free from the love of money." Ephesians 4:3 encourages us to "make every effort to keep the unity of the Spirit." And Luke 12:35 says, "Keep your lamps burning."

There are some things that God wants us to do ourselves. Yes, there are things that only He can do, but keeping the garbage out of our lives is our responsibility.

3. Realize you have the power to do it.

I've heard people say, "But I just don't have the strength to do it." Sorry, but based on God's Word you do have that strength and power. It isn't by human wit or grit, or by some self-styled ingenuity, but by a reliance on and dependence upon the Lord. We have that strength in the inner man, just as God promised.

> I pray that out of his glorious riches he may strengthen you with power through his Spirit in your inner being, so that Christ may dwell in your hearts through faith. And

I pray that you, being rooted and established in love, may have power, together with all the saints, to grasp how wide and long and high and deep is the love of Christ (Ephesians 3:16-18).

In that same chapter Paul goes on to tell us God is able to do immeasurably more than all we can ask or even imagine, according to His power that is at work within us. Picture that for a moment—God's strength is at work in you. With His power flowing through you, you have the strength to fight Satan and get the garbage out of your life, no matter how long it has been there.

We are told in 2 Peter 1:3 that God's divine power has given us everything we need for life and godliness. God's power is in you. That's why the apostle Paul could say, "I can do everything through him who gives me strength" (Philippians 4:13).

John, in his first epistle, says, "The one who is in you is greater than the one who is in the world" (1 John 4:4). The fact is, we have all the power and strength at our disposal we need to pull off a successful housecleaning. All we need to do is draw from that power.

4. Speak clearly to the devil in terms he understands.

We are told in two places in the New Testament that we are to "resist" the devil (James 4:7; 1 Peter 5:9). We also have the example of Jesus speaking to Satan when the Lord was tempted in the wilderness. You can speak to the devil that same way. Be very clear about this, Satan doesn't want you to do a housecleaning. As long as the garbage is in your life, he has a foot hold and can use it effectively to keep you bound in sin and unfruitful for Christ.

Sometimes you just need to look at the devil and say, "Satan, I resist and rebuke you as I now throw out of my life all the junk you've put there. Though you put it there, I'm pitching it out! Your plans have been canceled for me, your designs are disgusting, your deception is doomed, your effectiveness is eroding, your battle for my soul is lost, and your goal for my life is shot down. As I rid my life of all that is lewd, loveless, and lousy, I openly rebuke your power, your slyness, your influence, your ingenuity, and your victory in my life. By Jesus' blood, and by the authority of the empty tomb, I command you to get out of my way, as I pitch out forever all the junk I have allowed you to place there. My life is under new management now, and there is no place for you. Satan, I resist you and rebuke you as I clean the junk out of my life. By the blood of Jesus and by the authority of His empty tomb, I command you to leave, and officially cancel your ability to defeat me again!"

If you haven't said something like that to Satan, it's time you did. It'll help you get your house clean, and move you back on track.

5. Add accountability to your housecleaning list.

You need a trusted friend who will hold your feet to the fire as you do your housecleaning. Wise Solomon said it well:

Two are better than one, because they have a good return for their work: If one falls down, his friend can help him up. But pity the man who falls and has no one to help him up! Also, if two lie down together, they will keep warm. But how can one keep warm alone? Though one may be overpowered, two can defend themselves. A cord of three strands is not quickly broken (Ecclesiastes 4:9-12).

An accountability partner brings strength and encouragement to the process of housecleaning, and helps you remember to keep it clean in the future.

110

6. Make sure the cleaned space is refurnished with the right things.

Jesus once told a parable about an evil spirit that comes out of a man who just had a good housecleaning. In Matthew 12 the Lord explained that the evil spirit goes through arid places seeking rest, but finds none. So that demon decides to return to the house from which he came. When he arrives, he finds the house swept clean and put in order, so he goes and finds seven other spirits more wicked than himself to join him in the house. Jesus explained the final condition of that man is worse than when he started. That man should not only have cleaned up his home, he should have made sure to keep it clean. Of course, the Lord's parable isn't really about a man's house, but his life. Repentance will cause you to turn to God, but if you let your guard down you are susceptible to the same sins all over again.

You may sweep the junk out of your life, but unless you replace it with God's Word and prayer, it will fill up again with the same junk. That's why you must get the Word of Christ in your heart and let it do its work.

Is a housecleaning long overdue in your life? Then get to work cleaning. Don't try to house clean alone. God is your strength; rely on Him. And build in accountability from another person who will be honest and committed enough to ask the hard questions. We need each other. Maybe this is why James tells us to "confess [our] sins to each other" (James 5:16). Let another guy be a witness as you sweep out the junk that needs to go. Why not start right now? You'll be so glad you did!

Getting Back on Track

Is your life in need of a housecleaning?

What needs to be cleaned out?

According to Scripture, do you have the power to do it?

Have you ever talked to Satan the way this chapter suggests?

Who is holding you accountable in your walk with Christ?

With what would you like to fill your life, now that it is clean?

Chapter Twelve

Keys to Staying on Track

THIS BOOK HAS BEEN ABOUT *getting* back on track, and hopefully you have been encouraged to begin that process. But what about *staying* on track once you're back on? It's easier to get back on track than it is to stay there.

Someone has said that in the Old Testament, the Hebrews brought dead sacrifices and placed them on the altar. But under the New Covenant, we are now living sacrifices, according to Romans 12:1. The only problem with a "living" sacrifice is that it keeps crawling off the altar! We've all been frustrated with our lives getting off track, and it seems it's the same old sins that plague us again and again. So now that we're back on track, how do we stay there?

I believe the Scripture holds some keys for staying on track so that you won't keep feeling as though you've run off the rails. Keep these principles in mind as you continue to walk with Christ.

1. Realize who you are in Christ.

Maybe you're saying, "That's so obvious." I believe we often fall away because we've forgotten who we are in Christ. In other words, we have an identity crisis. What do I mean by "who we are in Christ"? Think about it.

- We are sons of God with all rights and privileges thereto attached (see Galatians 3:26).
- We're more than conquerors through Him who loved us (see Romans 8:37).
- We are heirs of God and fellow heirs with Christ (see Romans 8:17).
- We're justified from our sins (see Romans 5:1).
- We're new creations in Christ (see 2 Corinthians 5:17).
- We're washed and sanctified by the blood of Christ (see 1 Corinthians 6:9-11).
- We are sealed with the promised Holy Spirit (see Ephesians 1:13).
- We are seated with Christ in the heavenly realms (see Ephesians 2:6).
- We're united with Him in death (see Romans 6:5).
- We're gifted by the Holy Spirit (see 1 Peter 4:10).
- We're reconciled and saved forever (see Romans 5:10).
- We are fully forgiven of all sin (see Ephesians 1:7).
- We're free from all condemnation (see Romans 8:1).
- We're secure in our salvation forever (see John 10:28-29).

The list could go on and on, but enough references have been given to let you know you count. You are important and valuable to God—so valuable that He was willing to send His Son to die on the cross for you, so that He can have a relationship with you for all eternity. Once we were not a people, and

114

now we are God's people! If this is who we are, it should give us confidence to know we can stay on track. It's not impossible!

2. Claim God's promises when you are tempted.

The closer you get to the Lord, the greater will be your temptation. The devil is sure to come, for he wants to defeat you. You will never have a time in your life when you will not experience temptation. You can fight it off in two ways: either rely on the strength of your own flesh, or rely on the promise of God's Word. Personally, I trust the strength of God's Word over the strength of my own flesh.

Paul gave us an important truth in 1 Corinthians 10:13:

> No temptation has seized you except what is common to man. And God is faithful; he will not let you be tempted beyond what you can bear. But when you are tempted, he will also provide a way out, so that you can stand up under it.

I'm glad I learned that verse early in my Christian walk. It has kept me from many a yielding in my life time. It assures me that everyone experiences temptation, it asserts that God won't allow the temptation to be irresistible, and it promises me that He will provide a way out. It doesn't get any better than that.

Jesus fought temptation with the Word of God. We need to do the same. When God designed the Christian life, He did so with victory in mind, not defeat. Unfortunately, we're living in the kind of culture where sin abounds on every side. Satan is still like a roaring lion seeking whom he may devour (see 1 Peter 5:8). Someone has said that Christians walking around in their culture can be compared to someone walking through a lion's den. There is nothing that can insulate us against being surrounded by the lure and the pull to do the ungodly thing, but there is a power that can see us safely through.

3. Never fall into the trap of being over-confident.

Christians who have run off the track didn't wake up one morning and say, "I think I'll fall off the track today. I think I'll louse up my life by falling into sin." Instead, they thought they were doing fine. They thought they were above all that sin business, and Satan sneaked up on them. The subtlety of sin comes when your guard is down. No wonder Paul said, "So, if you think you are standing firm, be careful that you don't fall" (1 Corinthians 10:12).

The most dangerous and vulnerable time in your Christian walk is right after you've experienced a major victory. There is a surge of confidence that comes over you and says, "I'm invincible, I'm strong, I'm determined." Maybe that is why Paul, in urging the Galatians to restore those who have fallen, issues the stern warning: "But watch yourself, or you also may be tempted" (Galatians 6:1). That's wise advice. Paul added that because he knew even the most mature believer in Christ can get over-confident. That's all Satan needs to invade and do his work.

Of course, as a believer, you need to have confidence—and a lot of it. But it isn't self confidence, it's Christ-confidence. Remember the words of Paul to the believers at Corinth: "Such confidence as this is ours through Christ before God. Not that we are competent in ourselves to claim anything for ourselves, but our competence comes from God" (2 Corinthians 3:4-5).

A good example of pride and over-confidence is Uzziah in the Old Testament. Second Chronicles offers a glowing list of his great accomplishments, but at the end of the impressive list it says, "His fame spread far and wide, for he was greatly helped until he became powerful. But after Uzziah became powerful his pride led to his downfall" (26:15b-16). What a sad commentary on a man that accomplished much, but forgot to give God the credit and became over-confident in his own ability. If it can happen to Uzziah, it can happen to you. It was said many years ago, but is still true: Eternal vigilance is the price of freedom.

116

4. Stay filled with the Holy Spirit.

As a Christian, we dare not overlook the message of Ephesians 5: "Do not get drunk on wine, which leads to debauchery. Instead, be filled with the Spirit" (v. 18). This apostolic command was given to believers, not unbelievers. When you were saved, you received the gift of the Holy Spirit. It was at that point you were baptized in the Holy Spirit and sealed with the Spirit. As a Christian, you are now commanded to be filled with the Holy Spirit. What does that mean? First, the command is in the present, on-going sense: "Be constantly filled with the Holy Spirit." In Acts we see repeated fillings for empowerment. It doesn't mean we get more of the Holy Spirit, but that He finally gets all of us. To be filled with the Holy Spirit is to be controlled by the Holy Spirit. It means He is not only "resident" in us, He's "president" in us. It means that you have allowed him to sit in the driver's seat of your life, and it happens by a simple prayer you can say:

Spirit of God, fill me with you. I relinquish control of every room and every area of my life to you. I surrender all my ambition, all my will, and all my desires to you. I give my total loyalty to your sovereign will. Amen.

The Spirit of God will honor a heartfelt prayer and fill your life.

5. Practice spiritual warfare.

God's people are at war. Christianity is played out on the battleground, not the playground. We're not tourists, we're soldiers. Unless we realize the magnitude of the battle, great damage will be done.

Warfare begins with identifying the enemy. Satan is your enemy. The people who tempt you and pull you down are not the enemy, but victims of the enemy. Our struggle isn't really with them, it goes deeper and farther than that. Paul tells us, "Our struggle is not against flesh and blood, but against the rulers, against the authorities, against the powers of this dark

117

world and against the spiritual forces of evil in the heavenly realms" (Ephesians 6:12).

Our battle isn't fought on a human level, with human beings, in a human way, or with human weaponry. It's a spiritual battle, waged in a spiritual realm. Our arsenal is different than the world's. "For though we live in the world, we do not wage war as the world does. The weapons we fight with are not the weapons of the world" (2 Corinthians 10:3-4).

This calls for defensive and offensive tactics, which are spelled out for us in Ephesians 6: the belt of truth, the breast-plate of righteousness, the shoes of the gospel of peace, the shield of faith, the helmet of salvation, and the sword of the Spirit, which is the Word of God (see vv. 13-17). Paul ends that passage with an urgent plea to "pray in the Spirit on all occasions" (6:18). You can't fight cancer with aspirin and home remedies. Lethal situations call for lethal warfare. If we're fighting a supernatural enemy, we need to draw from a supernatural arsenal.

I've found it helpful many mornings, even before I get out of bed, to begin putting on that armor, piece by piece, claiming God's supernatural power to help me face my day. It's not a bad idea when you consider what is happening today in our world. Even when Jesus met temptation, He reached into God's arsenal and brought out the Word of God with which He neutralized all the flaming darts of the evil one. It worked for Him, and it will work for you.

6. Through prayer and fasting.

You don't hear much today about fasting, yet in the Bible it's mentioned many times. There is power in fasting, as one of the spiritual disciplines that keep us on track. Fasting was done in the Bible for many reasons. It brings the flesh under control of our spirit (see Leviticus 23:27), it helps us avert danger (see 2 Samuel 12:16; Ezra 8:21-23; Esther 4:16; 2 Chronicles 20:1-3), it can help us clarify God's direction for our lives (see

Judges 20:26-28; Acts 9:9-19; Acts 13:2-3), and there are times it may cancel or delay God's judgment (see 1 Kings 21:27-29).

Jesus fasted forty days and forty nights as He began His three-and-a-half-year ministry. Fasting does some great things for us. It deprives us for awhile of what, in fact, is a necessity to live—food. It confirms that our hunger for God is greater than our hunger for food for a period of time. It has become a bit of a lost discipline, but it can bring depth to your walk with God.

Prayer goes along with fasting. You can pray without fasting, but it's not a good idea to try fasting without praying. Different people fast for different lengths. Some fast for a twenty-four-hour period once every week or month. Others fast for three days or even seven days, and some have gone on a thirty-day fast. I suggest you consult your doctor if you fast for more than one day. In most cases it isn't dangerous, but you need to be physically and emotionally prepared before entering into a long fast. If you have never fasted, you're in for a spiritual high you will never forget.

May this prayer become your prayer as, with courage, you get back on track and stay on track with Jesus Christ:

A Prayer for Courage

God, give me courage—courage to stand, speak, go the distance, pay the price, take the risk, and take the flack. Give me courage to live by your truth instead of what's easy; to place principle above popularity, conviction above convenience, and right above recognition.

God, give me courage to be confident in the face of criticism, brave in the midst of barrage, assured in the onslaught of attack, dedicated at the time of decision, and focused in the moment of fire. Give me courage to say yes when everyone else is saying no; courage to follow when the majority scatters; courage to keep marching when the rest are meandering; courage to go when the crowd says stay; courage to walk when others just talk; courage to hope when many just cope; courage to contend when others pretend; courage to express instead of acquiesce; courage to shout when most just doubt; courage to stay the course, hold the line, finish the race, complete the journey, and never cave in.

Give me courage to be the maverick, set the pace, carry the torch, be called the fool, be laughed at, scorned, ridiculed, hated, written off, abused, or ignored. But let that courage keep me at my post, lifting high your truth, your standard, your Word, and your promise. Give me courage to not jump ship, bail out, run away, be intimidated, forsake the call, cave in, compromise, cow-tow, or run.

God, give me courage to dream big dreams, see large visions, plow new ground, chart new courses, sail new seas, and set new records. Give me courage to put character above compromise, purity above popularity, resolve above relevance, passion above pleasure, and faithfulness above flippancy.

God, give me courage to think your thoughts, obey your commands, follow your path, take the guff, suffer the loss, carry your cross, and be your faithful disciple—clear to the end. Amen.

It's time to get back on track!

Getting Back on Track

Take a few minutes to write out who the Bible says you are in Christ.

How does Satan attack you?

How can you fight off his attacks?

What does it mean to be filled with the Spirit?

In what ways are you in a spiritual battle?

How can you best prepare for the battle?